ART AS I

ART AS POLITICS

THE FUTURE OF ART AND COMMUNITY

ADAM MICHAEL KRAUSE

Art as Politics:
The Future of Art and Community

ISBN 978-82-93064-14-5
ISBN 978-82-93064-54-1
ISBN 978-82-93064-15-2 (ebook)

Published by New Compass Press
Grenmarsvegen 12,
N–3912 Porsgrunn,
Norway

Design and layout by Eirik Eiglad

New Compass presents ideas on participatory democracy, social ecology, and movement building—for a free, secular, and ecological society.

new-compass.net
2011

TABLE OF CONTENTS

AUTHOR'S PREFACE

Leo Tolstoy, near the end of *What Is Art?*, states:

> I have accomplished, to the best of my ability, this work which has occupied me for fifteen years, on a subject near to me - that of art. By saying that this subject has occupied me for fifteen years, I do not mean that I have been writing this book fifteen years, but only that I began to write on art fifteen years ago, thinking that when once I undertook the task I should be able to accomplish it without a break. It proved, however, that my views on the matter were so far from clear that I could not arrange them in a way that satisfied me. [...] Now I have finished it; and however badly I have performed the task, my hope is that my fundamental thought as to the false direction

> the art of our society has taken and is following, as to the reasons of this, and as to the real destination of art, is correct, and that therefore my work will not be without avail.[1]

My own experiences writing about art are frighteningly similar. Although I did not spend fifteen years writing this book, it *was* conceived nearly a decade ago, attempted, abandoned, reconceived, and reattempted, only to be abandoned and reconceived again. And like Tolstoy, my views on art were not sufficiently clear when I first began. The very process of writing forced me to rethink most of my positions on the subject. As I wrote, my views became not only more clear and consistent, but increasingly radical as well. Had I finished what I first conceived, I would have written a fairly ordinary book about art with a few contrarian elements and maybe a complaint or two about the negative impacts of commerce on the arts. Through my reading, writing and rewriting, I have come to regard the current role of the arts in our society with what could safely be called "outright contempt," and the tone and content of what follows certainly reflects that. If I sometimes seem overly strident, that is simply the unavoidable impact that mounting disillusionment has on my prose.

Portions of this book were previously published in the journals *Social Anarchism* and *Communalism*, and I am grateful for the permission to reprint what originally graced their pages.

Several people read this book in manuscript form, and offered many helpful suggestions. First, I need to thank Jason Gubbels, who has read and edited nearly everything I have ever written without complaint or pay. The quality of his suggestions, coupled with his incredible command of the English language, has never ceased to amaze and humble me. Natalie Taber read an early draft, and was instrumental in transforming the sections on John Dewey into a far more interesting bit of writing. As I prepared the final draft, Erin Wolf was a very valuable accomplice. She provided a number of useful suggestions for improving the Introduction, and helped turn it into something that might actually compel readers to forge ahead into what follows.

Finally, I need to thank Eirik Eiglad at *New Compass*, who not only believed in this project from the moment it was presented to him, but played the role of editor magnificently. His comments were invariably insightful, and he refused to accept any less than the best I could muster. His involvement and encouragement made it possible to bring this book to its finished form.

Of course, all remaining errors, both those of omission and commission, are mine alone.

Adam Krause
February 1, 2011

INTRODUCTION

The arts currently serve the needs of the free market, not the needs of human beings. The central goals of the free market are accumulation and growth—goals which the arts have been falsely forced to serve. The arts have other values—from creating and sharing meaning, to transforming and elevating the materials of the world—that are far more important than profitability. By serving the needs of the free market, the arts have largely been prevented from realizing these other values. Art's worth *as art* cannot be fully expressed, nor can humanity's cultural needs be met, when capitalist demands drive the production of art.

The free market has degraded and devalued the arts in two distinct ways. First, the capitalist culture industry has managed to commandeer control over all but a tiny fraction of the art and music that constitutes our shared cultural experience, and sells commodified cultural products *into* society, rather than allowing art to emanate *from* society. Second, high art has been roped off in museums, or placed only in the hands of the exceptionally wealthy. In either case, the arts come with a price tag, and enter day-to-day experience as if from an outside realm, whether handed down from the seats of monetary power and placed in the marketplace, or declared an untouchable specimen of artistic greatness that one must make a special trip to see.

Art ought to be inextricably bound to its role and function in the lives of individuals and cultures. But in our culture, it operates in an untenable way. Rather than being an integral element in the collective life of an organized community, the arts have either been commodified into irrelevance and inefficacy or turned into a roped-off diversion.

The arts are not alone in being hampered by a capitalist context. Many of the same elements that have contributed to art's current dysfunction have similarly corrupted our social, political, and ecological realms. By making business' bottom line the measure of any success or failure, our interactions, goals, and ambitions in every facet of our lives have taken on unhealthy and unnatural dimensions.

As will be shown, the solutions to our artistic problems, our social problems, our political problems, and our ecological problems, have related causes and related solutions. It will be further demonstrated that an artistically radical project, intimately entwined in a politically radical project, is our only escape from the confines of the present.

Our relationship with art needs to be rethought, restructured and replaced. For art to function well, our systems for producing and distributing art must be transformed in truly profound and radical ways. Art needs to operate on a human scale, under the control of the people who make, distribute, and appreciate it, so that it can play a role in the collective life of healthy, functioning communities.

CORPORATE CONTROL OF ART

Corporate intrusion into the arts is one of the main causes of art's current dysfunction. By turning art into an article of trade that needs to sell well in order to have value, art becomes a mere commodity rather than a source of value or meaning. By making the business of show business the central focus of artistic production, the arts are rendered just another disposable commodity whose function is to line the pockets of the corporate culture industry.

The continuing encroachment of corporate culture into music is an especially pernicious instance of business pulling art out of its proper context. This corporate control, though going through fundamental changes, remains strong. The rise of the Internet and the digitization of music have eroded the power of record labels, often large conglomerates who had managed to not only package and sell music, but had also attached an extra layer of marketers, managers and other marginally talented entities onto music in order to profit. Brian Eno, in a 2010 interview, compared the demise of the record industry in the twentieth century to the collapse of the whale blubber industry of the nineteenth:

> I think records were just a bubble through time and those who made a living from them for a while were lucky. There is no reason why anyone should have made so much money from selling records except that everything was right for this period of time. I always knew it would run out sooner or later. It couldn't last and now it's running out. I don't particularly care that it is and like the way things are going. The record age was just a blip. It was a bit like if you had a source of whale blubber in the 1840s and it could be used as fuel. Before gas came along, if you traded in whale blubber, you were the richest man on Earth. Then gas came along and you'd be stuck with your whale blubber. Sorry mate—history's moving along.[2]

The erosion of record labels has created a vacuum into which artists can step and regain control over the creation and distribution of music. Thanks to increasingly affordable home recording equipment as well as the distributive powers of the Internet, it is altogether possible to record and disseminate music on a global scale at very little cost.

However, rather than just fueling greater artistic control, the erosion of the record industry has also allowed other corporations—everyone from creators of shoes to soft drinks—to move into the vacuum left by record labels, thus reasserting corporate control over music before other systems could fully develop. In October 2010, The New York Times reported on this new corporate encroachment.[3] The story centered on Converse, a shoe company founded in the early years of the twentieth century and recently acquired by Nike.[4] Converse plans to open a recording studio in Brooklyn where it will record bands for free in exchange for Converse-sponsored compilation appearances, the public display of Converse-festooned feet, and just basically allowing a shoe company to draw on the hip cache of so-called "independent" music.

Converse is by no means alone in this—its parent company, Nike, has released musical compilations. The hyper-caffeinated soft drinks Red Bull and Mountain Dew have their own record labels. Mountain Dew's Green Label Sounds has released free mp3s of new work by various, often highly respected bands. By paying for such things as recording, video shoots, production, or distribution, these corporations act as patrons of the arts, assuming the role currently being vacated by record labels. These corporations use their associations with bands to help "brand" their companies, while simultaneously prolonging corporate control of music. The willing complicity of so many artists in this corporate sponsorship, along with the lack of outcry in the "independent" music community, are troubling symptoms of a persistent problem.[5]

For art to serve its purpose—or rather, purposes—it must be radically situated within the life of a community and under the control of ordinary people. Corporate control needs to be sloughed off once and for all. Art must be decentralized and democratized. There ought to be numerous creative activities performed by numerous individuals that seek, not for the artist to succeed in the capitalist culture industry, or to appear in a glossy art magazine, but for the artist and all those who gather around the creation and dissemination of artworks to add value to the shared experience of their community.

DEFINING THE DEBATE

We sit at an interesting juncture in our cultural history. Following the ascendance of the Internet, the control of the production and distribution of the arts is up for grabs. It could again be possible to create and share works on a human scale. The capitalist culture industry will do everything in its formidable powers to maintain dominance, but its success is by no means assured. This is particularly true if a concerted effort is mounted on a community level to place the control of culture in human hands.

We need revitalized and reinvigorated politically motivated art. The majority of previous political art has sadly settled for half-measures or simply resigned itself to the role of an accepted, marginalized, dissenting voice. Art must aid in the creation of viable *counter*cultures, rather than simply *sub*cultures that are allowed to exist as tolerated fringes posing no real threat to existing cultural and political institutions. Subcultures can certainly facilitate the partial liberation of a handful of individuals, but what ultimately matters is the liberation of society as a whole.

In a moment, we will turn to John Dewey's *Art As Experience*, a book that provides a description of art grounded in human life and experience. Rather than working from a hallowed canon of various masterpieces to create his description of art, Dewey wisely defines art through its role in everyday reality. There are ideas implicit in Dewey's description of art that are made explicit in the German artist Joseph Beuys' thoughts and activities. Beuys claimed that "Everyone is an artist." He did not mean that everyone is currently an artist in the conventional sense, nor did he mean that everyone should take up painting or sculpting, but rather, that creativity and the ability to reimagine and reconstruct the world are *the* central facets of humanity's uniqueness. If every realm of experience could be approached artistically and creatively, it could be possible to enact what Beuys called "social sculpture"—a creative reconfiguration of every aspect of life.

By following Dewey and Beuys, it is possible to provide an account of art and creativity that is intimately tied to the development of a more decentralized, non-hierarchical, and truly democratic social order.

John Cage's musical practices, which often make use of form as a demonstration of alternative social and political practices will also be discussed at length, as these ideas further develop some of the possible applications of the politically transformative power of art. Cage's notions are particularly important for creating politically efficacious art in our current milieu. Because the very language of resistance and revolution has been adopted by corporations and advertising agencies, simply *demanding* political change through art is not enough. The auto manufacturer Dodge invited everyone to "Join the Dodge Rebellion." Burger King claimed that "Sometimes You Gotta Break the Rules." No less a subcultural hero and symbol of subversion than William Burroughs appeared in a Nike ad. The slogans and signifiers of rebellion and resistance have become the common parlance of advertisers and transnational corporations.

Art that just *talks* about rebellion and resistance will almost inevitably be drowned out when car companies and fast food restaurants preposterously push their products as a source of subversion. New means of resisting the corporate stranglehold over the world—besides merely talking about it—need to be developed, both in the arts and elsewhere. Cage attempted to use his music to *show*—rather than simply *say*—how the world could be different.[6] Art and music like Cage's, that actually embodies better modes of being, offers a possible source of viable cultural resistance.

Beyond these Cagean concerns about the political ramifications of an artwork's formal structure, there also need to be cultural institutions that operate beyond the confines of the culture industry. By offering an alternate system for distributing and consuming art, these institutions could constitute a cultural counterpower that could challenge and replace the capitalist culture industry. The goal should not be to simply operate *outside* the culture industry, but to supplant it.

If art created by these new institutions is to serve a truly useful purpose, our social and political realms will need to be similarly transformed. In order to fully succeed, this decommodified art will need a similarly decommodified social context in which to operate. By creating and demonstrating new modes of being and interacting, artistic change *can* work in advance of political change. But ultimately, artistic change and political change need to work in tandem, or else this decommodified and revolutionized art will be left without a proper context to function.

Having established how art *ought to* work, it will be possible to delve into recent art theory in the form of modernism and postmodernism. The modernists described art history as a series of formal developments that move teleologically toward a single end. The modernist account of art is ultimately an intricately woven historical fiction that ignores the true complexity of the art world in favor of a reductive and exclusionary tale that pushes to the perimeter anything that does not fit into its tidy boundaries. Postmodernists adopted the basic tenets of this reductive and inaccurate framework, and made a new series of errors regarding the role and function of art.

Throughout the discussion of modernism and postmodernism, particular attention will be paid to their respective accounts of artistic progress. The modernists created a very peculiar definition of artistic progress, and the postmodernists in turn rejected *artistic progress in general* through the dismissal of the modernists' very peculiar notion. As will be shown, neither camp's account is accurate. Both work from a flawed description of art, which the modernists derived in part from Immanuel Kant's aesthetic theories, and conclude with an equally flawed version of artistic progress. Luckily, a better account of what might constitute artistic progress exists, an ecological version based upon progress as experienced in the natural world. This ecological account of artistic progress is one of the key facets in a new description of art that can aid in the creative reconstruction of not only art, but the political realm as well.

The account of art that follows from the work and ideas of Dewey, Beuys, and Cage stands in diametric opposition to these schools of thought. Hopefully, by showing the inherent weaknesses and misunderstandings of art inherent to modernism and postmodernism, it will become readily apparent that a new understanding of art and its role in society must replace them.

ART AS MEANINGFUL EXPERIENCE

Before we can assess the importance of art in social life, we must first determine just what art is, how it works, why it is important, and why humans create it in the first place. John Dewey's *Art As Experience*, though published in 1934, still constitutes one of the best available descriptions of art and its proper role in human life, and provides a radical, far-reaching account of art's function.

Art As Experience deserves an in-depth investigation at the outset of our discussion, as it details a description of the arts that is linked to everyday experience. This will lay the groundwork for understanding much of what follows. Art may have changed and expanded a great deal since 1934, both in the introduction of new media and in an expanded concept of what may constitute an artwork, but Dewey's basic thesis can be applied to any of these new developments without significant alteration.

According to Dewey, art has been separated from life. This dichotomy between art and life tears art away from the only context in which it could properly function, namely, human life. As will be seen, there are no compelling reasons to separate art from life. In fact, both become richer and fuller when understood as part of a single continuum. The unity between art and life becomes especially apparent when one considers art's genesis. Art arose from the rituals and practices of everyday life. As Dewey states,

> Dancing and pantomime, the sources of the art of the theatre, flourished as a part of religious rites and celebrations. Musical art abounded in the fingering of stretched string, the beating of the taught skin, the blowing with reeds. Even in the caves, human habitations were adorned with colored pictures that kept alive to the senses experiences with the animals that were so closely bound with the lives of humans. Structures that housed their gods and the instrumentalities that facilitated commerce with the higher powers were wrought with especial fineness. But the arts of the drama, music, painting, and architecture thus exemplified had no particular connection with theatres, galleries, museums. They were part of the significant life of an organized community.[7]

In short, art arose from everyday experience, and should still be a part of that experience.

Dewey could be accused of degrading and materializing art, but such is not the case. Art plays a vital role in human life in Dewey's conception, a role that is, in fact, much greater than if it were placed apart from lived experience. Art should not be an entity that one *leaves life* to encounter, but should, rather, be an integral element of that life. By insisting that art and life should be closely connected, Dewey does not degrade art, but rather, demonstrates the conditions in which it might flourish.

Because there ought to be no separation between art and life, Dewey resists beginning his description of art with the commonly accepted canon of masterpieces, so as to describe art through the frequently-held traits of such works. Instead, he begins with life, and an account of what experience is. From there, he places artworks within the context of that experience, demonstrates how they emanate from and enrich that experience, and how experience in turn enriches our understanding of art.

If art is part of experience, it seems fitting to ask, "What is experience?" Dewey has a peculiar definition of the term, as he makes a distinction between *an* experience and experience in general. And it is this peculiar notion of *an* experience that is essential to his description of art.

WHAT IS EXPERIENCE?

Life takes place in an environment, in relation, response, and interchange with it. Both the environment and the living creature constantly swing between states of equilibrium and disequilibrium, sometimes together, sometimes in opposition. There is much more than mere flux in this interchange between organism and environment. For Dewey, "form is arrived at whenever a stable, even though moving, equilibrium is reached."[8] The attainment of such a state of equilibrium then sets the stage for new struggles and interactions, and potentially, the attainment of a new state of equilibrium.

This is not a simple return to a prior state, but the creation of a new one. These moments, when a stable, but moving, form is reached, constitute for Dewey the act of "having an experience." The environment and the live creature have together been reconfigured in such a way that a sort of union has been reached. The tensions of the lived experience have been temporarily resolved, form has been created, and a new plateau has been reached where the organism may pause for a moment before embarking on a new struggle that may lead to new moments of resolution. As Dewey further elaborates on his notion of having *an* experience:

> A piece of work is finished in a way that is satisfactory; a problem receives its solution; a game is played through; a situation, whether that of eating a meal, playing a game of chess, carrying on a conversation, writing a book, or taking part in a political campaign, is so rounded out that its close is a consummation and not a cessation.[9]

It is such moments of having *an* experience that ideally take place during the creation and appreciation of art. Art is an encounter with an environment, an attempt to transform the materials at hand into a finished, stable form. Both acts, creation and appreciation, occur within the flow of life, through it, because of it, and in interaction with it. Art is the conversion of objective material into an intense and clear experience that occurs within the larger context of the interchange between organism and environment.

The various example of *an* experiences quoted above—Dewey's examples range from eating a meal to carrying out a political campaign—might seem to have very little to do with the act of painting a picture, writing a novel, composing a poem, or a symphony. But each of the activities Dewey discusses, when carried through to a consummation that closes and rounds out the process of partaking in it, becomes *an* experience. Art is, quite simply, another example of *an* experience. In the arts, as in other experiences, there is inception, development, and fulfillment that result in the completion of an integrated, dynamic whole. This conflation of art with experience does not cheapen or degrade either. Life can be as transformative as a profound artistic experience, and art can be as transformative as a profound life experience. *An* experience, whether in art or "ordinary" life, brings about the acquisition of a previously non-existent form and order.

AN AESTHETIC WORLD

Successful art is that which has been brought to completion as a dynamic whole that rounds out an experience for its creator, its viewer, or both. The materials at hand are reordered, rearranged, and most importantly, *elevated* into a new entity with a significance that the raw materials did not originally possess. Just like any other experience, the creation of art is a process that takes place over a period of time. This means much more than the simple fact that it takes time to put paint on a canvas or print words on a page. Rather, "the expression of the self in and through a medium, constituting the work of art, is *itself* a prolonged interaction of something issuing from the self with objective conditions, a process in which both of them acquire a form and order they did not at first possess."[10] The act of creation occurs through a series of experimental interchanges that arrive, after a lengthy process, at the finished work.

If one began with a full conception of the completed work, then the act of creation would not be a truly worthwhile interaction with the materials of one's environment. In such an instance, one would not be aiming towards the creation of a previously non-existent state of equilibrium, but would instead be squeezing the materials at hand into an already existent form. As Dewey states, "If one examines into the reason why certain works of art offend us, one is likely to find that there is no personally felt emotion guiding the selecting and assembling of the materials presented. [...] We are irritated by a feeling that he is manipulating materials to secure an effect decided upon in advance."[11] Further, "we are repelled by the intrusion of moral design in literature while we aesthetically accept any amount of moral content if it is held together by a sincere emotion that controls the material."[12] Art, if it is to succeed, needs to be created through a process of interaction between artist and environment. This interaction should seek to resolve the tensions of lived experience, but not in a pre-ordained manner. *An* experience results in the creation of a new form, not from rehashing an existent one.

Obviously, Dewey's description of art does not actually supply a *definition* of art. The boundary between what is and what is not art remains inchoate. *Successful* artworks create *an* experience. But what about unsuccessful artworks that fail to do so? Are these still works of art? What about objects and events that create *an* experience but fall beyond the commonly-held boundaries of art? Are these just experientially similar to successful artworks? Or by succeeding where many attempted artworks fail, do such objects and events attain the status of art?

There are two obvious, but divergent, ways out of this confusion. In the first solution to this conundrum, we accept that while there are many unsuccessful artworks that fail to create *an* experience, these failed attempts remain artworks nonetheless, while many objects and events that create *an* experience, and are thus experientially similar to successful artworks, remain beyond the bounds of art. In this first solution, it would be up to each society to *ad hoc* its way to a working definition of what is and what is not art. The border would remain nebulous.

The second, far more radical, solution involves expanding the definition of art to include anything that creates *an* experience. A political campaign carried to a satisfying conclusion, or a conversation that brings definition to a formerly vague idea, may be so experientially similar to successful artworks that these things may as well be deemed a form of art. Dewey says a great deal throughout

Art As Experience which ultimately suggests that he holds this second, more radical, view. On numerous occasions he discusses the aesthetic qualities of all true experiences, eventually stating, "Any practical activity will, provided that it moves by its own urge to fulfillment, have aesthetic quality."[13] *All* true experiences organize the materials of the world into a stable, finished form with an aesthetic quality. This is also Dewey's description of art: it organizes the materials of the world into a stable, finished form with an aesthetic quality. Nowhere does he make a clear distinction between art in particular and *an* experience in general, and it seems safe to assume that Dewey sees all instances of *an* experience as art.

That art takes its nature from the very process of living is not at all surprising. Were the arts a completely separate set of activities with no relation to any other facets of life, the arts would have no foundation on which to rest. For Dewey, the creation of art is simply part of the general human drive to expand and enrich life by reordering and restructuring the materials at hand into a more satisfactory form. That there is an overlap between the various manifestations of that drive is not at all surprising.

EVERYONE IS AN ARTIST

The German artist Joseph Beuys took this very idea, that our understanding of art ought to be expanded to include any activity deliberately executed to create a previously non-existent form, and made it central to his thought. Beuys famously stated that "Everyone is an artist." He did not mean that everyone currently *is* an artist, but that everyone has the creative potential to transform the materials of the world in previously unimagined ways. As Beuys claimed, "The most radical and probably only sensible thing would be to bring the artistic into consciousness and make it clear that man cannot live without it."[14] Beuys decreed that life is properly lived as a creative activity with the world as its material. *Real* art, in Beuys' conception, has yet to be achieved. The ultimate art form is a social *gesamtkuntswerk* (total artwork), which he called "social sculpture," a creative reshaping of humanity and society that would utilize the untapped artistry of everyone to create new political structures.

For an early exhibition in 1965, Beuys sat in front of his drawings, his head covered in honey and gold-leaf, while he quietly explained his drawings to a dead rabbit cradled in his arms. Entitled *How to Explain Pictures to a Dead Hare*, this work introduced honey as a potent symbol in Beuys' work.[15] Just as honey is the product of bees, thoughts and new ideas—which come from the head[16]—are the products of humans. Beuys covered his head in honey to highlight this correlation. His mind made it possible to create and explain his works. And it is only by similarly unleashing humanity's collective creative potential that our greatest work, a social sculpture, could be created.

Beuys' art and thought are so idiosyncratic, and so tied to his biography, that his life, works, and thought cannot be adequately discussed in separation. He was born in Kleve, Germany in 1921. As a child, Beuys was fascinated by the natural sciences and planned on a career in medicine. But after WWII, his interests and ambitions changed. During the war, he flew for the Nazi Luftwaffe, and was shot down in Crimea in 1943. He was nursed back to health by a tribe of nomadic Tatars who wrapped him in fat and felt to keep him warm.[17] Beuys would later use fat and felt as materials in his art, with which he hoped to heal humanity much as the Tatars had healed him.[18] Fat and felt became part of a complex artistic code through which Beuys wished to point the way toward social solutions entirely opposed to the values of the Nazism for which he once flew.

Following the war, Beuys attended art school. In the early 1950s, he entered a near-decade of intense solitude and severe depression, punctuated in 1957 by a complete mental and physical collapse, apparently due to a combination of his wartime experiences, the aftermath of German fascism, and guilt over his role in it. Beuys emerged from this bout of depression with a very unique body of work, that, while rooted in his own experiences, sought to turn his personal rebirth into a collective one. As Beuys stated, "This social organism is so ill that it is absolutely high time to subject it to radical treatment, otherwise humanity will go under. And our social organism exists like a living being in a condition of the severest illness."[19]

Until his death in 1986, Beuys' art moved steadily from personal works with a political dimension to more explicitly political works still bearing his unique stamp. Notably, Beuys was also involved in a number of more conventionally political activities. In 1967, he founded the German Student Party, which demanded self-determination in law, culture, and economics. 1970 saw the formation of Non-Voters for Direct Democracy by Referendum, which sought to create citizens' initiatives that could set policy from below, rather than above. Beuys was also instrumental in founding the German Green Party.

Of particular importance in our present discussion of art's potential as a political force are Beuys' artworks from the last 20 years of his life, as these almost invariably utilize his expanded definition of art alongside his political ideas in such a way that art and the creative reconstruction of society are unified to an incredible degree. Two works in particular stand out from the flurry of activity that constitute this latter portion of Beuys' life and career, *Honey Pump at the Workplace* (1977) and *7000 Oaks* (1982).

At Documenta 6 in Kassel, Germany, Beuys installed a mechanical pump that circulated several tons of honey through tubes around the gallery space. But this represented only a portion of the sculpture. Its other facet was its human element. For 100 days, Beuys hosted talks and discussions led by artists, economists, leaders of citizens' initiatives, and various other individuals from around the world concerned with humanity's political and ecological future. With these various people circulating their ideas against the backdrop of honey in motion, *Honey Pump at the Workplace* functions similarly to *How to Explain Pictures to a Dead Hare*. There is, again, the correlation between honey as the product of bees and new ideas as the product of humanity. Just as honey is circulated around the space, so too are plans for sculpting and recreating society.

In Beuys' peculiar definition of capital, this circulation of new ideas—or art, in his expanded sense—is the spread of capital. He felt that capital is not money, but human creativity. The true value that humans add to the world does not come from the ability to fund and invest, but to invent and create. As such, art, for Beuys, *is* capital. As Beuys said in an interview conducted shortly after Documenta 6:

> Art is capital. This is not some pipe dream; it is reality. In other words, capital is what art is. Capital is human capacity and what flows from it. So there are only two organs involved here, or two polar relationships: creativity and human intention, from which a product arises. These are the real economic values, nothing else. Money is not. However, we have a concept of capital where an economic value intervenes and wrecks everything, which therefore makes the economy revolve around profit, exploitation, etc.[20]

Against the backdrop of his honey pump, Beuys put his "creative capital" into circulation, and thereby helped provide a step toward a path out of our present morass. Of course, Beuys' definition of capital is very unusual. It is not necessary to follow Beuys in substituting an expanded concept of art for "capital." What is worth noting are the implications of this proposed substitution. The worth of human activities should not be judged by monetary value, but by their value as activities in themselves, outside the confines of the market and the demands of business.

7000 Oaks, presented at Documenta 7 in Kassel, similarly included a moving, dynamic sculpture alongside a strong social element. Outside the building that housed Documenta 7, Beuys piled 7000 pieces of basalt in the form of an arrow, pointing toward a single oak tree. Over the course of the next five years, as 6,999 more oaks were planted in and around Kassel, the pieces of basalt were simultaneously removed from the pile and placed alongside each tree. Much like his sculptures with fat, which morph and evolve over time, *7000 Oaks* is an active, endlessly shifting work of art. Early in the tree's life, it is dwarfed by the stone. But as time passes, the tree slowly grows until it towers over it.

This collectively executed, ecologically minded, endlessly evolving work may seem like a stretch as "sculpture," but within the context of Beuys' expanded concept of art and his notion of social sculpture, *7000 Oaks* becomes not just *art*, but a powerful work that points to humanity's ability to creatively transform the world. It is also notable that even in this late work, completed after his life, Beuys was still grappling with the aftermath of Nazism. During WWII, the Nazis had appropriated the oak as a symbol of national pride. By using it in his work, Beuys reclaimed the oak for his own political project, pointing toward the future while refusing to lose sight of the past.

SOCIAL EXPERIENCE AND SOCIAL SCULPTURE

Beuys, much like John Dewey, believed that art is properly understood as an integral part of human life, not a separate, etherealized diversion from it. Moreover, both Beuys and Dewey presented an expanded concept of art, wherein art is not simply a collection of disciplines called "the arts," but is the practice of using creativity to transform the materials of the world into a new, more satisfactory form. For both, art and creativity possess a strong social dimension. In a passage in *Art As Experience*, Dewey states:

> Works of art that are not remote from common life, that are widely enjoyed in a community, are signs of a unified collective life. The remaking of the material of experience in the act of expression is not an isolated event confined to the artist and to a person here or there who happens to enjoy the work. In the degree in which art exercises its office, it is also a remaking of the experience of the community in the direction of greater order and unity.[21]

Dewey, in this passage, makes a point that seems to imply something *similar* to Beuys' social sculpture, but one should be cautious not to read Beuys' radical conclusions into this statement. Beuys takes the views he holds in common with Dewey to a far more radical conclusion and thus points to ways in which we can move beyond Dewey's groundwork, and add a more totalized social dimension to art and creativity. If art is defined as the creative reshaping of the world, it can be expanded in scope beyond its ordinary boundaries, to yield the logical conclusion that the principles involved in art and creativity can be used to radically overhaul our very ill social organism.

If art is to have a bearing on humanity's understanding of what is socially possible, it will be worth discussing some of the practical aspects involved in making art a socio-political force. Some of these practices center around the dissemination of art. Namely, who is fueling the production and distribution of art, and for what purpose? Is art a commodified diversion that fills the coffers of the culture industry? Or is art used as a source of shared value and meaning in thriving human communities?

Yet beyond these questions of economy and scale, there remains the issue of the formal aspects of art-as-art. Because the arts have the power to recreate and reorder experience, they offer a fertile staging ground for establishing new ways of seeing, thinking, and being. With a conscious effort toward the manner in which culture is made and disseminated, it is altogether possible to utilize art as an arena in which to test and develop new modes of social interaction. Once art has been taken back from the museum and the market, and placed in human hands in human communities, it holds the potential to fundamentally reorder and reconfigure those communities in new, previously unimagined ways. In a moment, we will turn to the music of John Cage, who developed means by which the experience of the artwork itself could have a powerful socio-political impact, and could aid in reordering and reconfiguring our communities.

ART AND FORMAL STRUCTURE

Using the formal elements of artworks to experientially model new social and political forms is one of the key ways in which art can aid in the creative reconstruction of society. This concept was carried out on numerous occasions by the American composer John Cage. Cage wanted to use his music "as a means of changing the mind."[22] Not simply his own mind, but the minds of the audience as well. His music put on display new forms of social interaction, allowing people to experience alternative social structures in an actual situation. In 1988 and 1989, Cage presented the Charles Eliot Norton Lectures at Harvard University. The lectures were later published in a book called *I-VI*. Along the bottom of each page, acting as a visual counterpoint to the main text, are excerpts from the question and answer periods.[23] On the bottom of page 176, Cage is asked if he believes his music to have political content or effect. He responds:

> I think one of the things that distinguishes music from the other arts is that music often requires other people. The performance of a piece of music is a public occasion or a social occasion. This brings it about that the performance of a piece of music can be a metaphor of society, of how we want society to be. Though we are not now living in a society which we consider good, we could make a piece of music in which we would be willing to live.[24]

Although Cage does not explicitly say this to his questioner, he did not see his music as having any kind of content, including political. In fact, Cage spent the majority of his career composing contentless music in which sounds could simply be sounds and would signify nothing beyond themselves. Yet, despite this intentional contentlessness, Cage's music still possesses an intended political *effect* in its formal structure and manner of presentation, in that, during the performance of the music, it is capable of establishing different types of relationships between people.

Cage, especially later in his career, attempted to put on display and in action a working model of a non-hierarchical, decentralized society. In his compositions and performances, he nearly always dispensed with a conductor, thus removing centralized authority from the performance, leaving only the musicians, operating as equals. Moreover, Cage composed the majority of his music through chance operations, which forced him to accept whichever sounds chance dictated, thereby allowing him to remove his own tastes and preferences from his compositions. He thus relinquished the traditional role of the composer and the power that such a role entails, and in turn became just another member of the audience, surprised by whatever sounds might happen to be played. In a 1957 essay, he writes, "one may give up the desire to control sound, clear his mind of music, and set about discovering means to let sounds be themselves rather than vehicles for man-made theories or expressions of human sentiments."[25]

If the sounds are there by chance, then no sound, instrument, or movement is by nature any more important than any other. Cage explains the significance of this in a conversation appearing on the Glenn Branca recording *Indeterminate Activity of Resultant Masses*:

> To be able to move one's attention from one point to another without feeling that one had left something important behind is the feeling that I enjoy having and which I hope to give to others. So that each person can place his attention originally rather than in a compelled way. So that each person is in charge of himself.[26]

For Cage, the composer, the sounds, and the performers are all presented as equals and the audience members are encouraged to place their attention anywhere. No one individual's will is forced upon anyone else's.

This personal autonomy in listening is evident throughout Cage's work in both minimal and maximal musical situations. *4'33"* (1952), perhaps Cage's most well-known work, consists of three completely silent movements whose duration adds up to the 4 minutes and 33 seconds of the title. Cage supplies an empty rhythmic structure that allows for any sound to occur and be accepted as the music. The nothingness he provides is not a nihilistic nothing, but a nothingness that leaves room for everything, and thus points to life as the ultimate source of aesthetic enjoyment. In his essay "Forerunners of Modern Music," Cage first posits rhythm, rather than harmony, as the ideal means for structuring music. He defines rhythm as "relationships of lengths of time."[27] He then goes on to say that "Any sounds of any qualities and pitches (known or unknown, definite or indefinite), any contexts of these, simple or multiple, are natural and conceivable within a rhythmic structure which equally embraces silence."[28] *4'33"* is a rhythmic structure (a series of durations) in which whatever sounds the listener chooses to give auditory attention become the piece.

The same holds true for *HPSCHD* (1967-69), a piece that would seem to be the polar opposite of *4'33*." *HPSCHD*, a collaboration with Lejaren Hiller, involves seven harpsichords and 51 tapes of pre-recorded music.

> These sonic resources were only a small part of a five-hour multimedia extravaganza, held in the University of Illinois Assembly Hall. The harpsichords were placed on platforms distributed around this enormous circular arena, and the loudspeakers were arranged around the perimeter of the dome. [...] Several thousand slides were displayed (by means of eighty projectors) on large transparent screens hung from the center of the arena; several films were also shown on these screens.

> Blacklights, spotlights, and a discothèque-style mirrored ball completed the visual side of the event. Some 7,000 people came to the show, milling about among the performers and taking in the sights and sounds.[29]

In *HPSCHD*, the abundance of stimuli makes the piece more than a single thing that everyone ought to experience in a predetermined manner. Audience members can come and go as they please, placing their attention in unique, non-compelled ways. *HPSCHD* is experienced on each listener's own time and terms. The listeners have full autonomy, taking in as much or as little of the piece as they desire. With pieces like *HPSCHD*, Cage provides a musical experience which discards the traditional notion that a piece of music occurs from point A to point B of linear time, and the assumption that anyone hearing the piece performed in this space of time has heard *the* piece. Instead, everyone is free to drop in or out at their own choosing, taking in as much or as little as they want, and having an experience of the piece unlike anyone else's.

Cage's music provides not only openness and freedom for the audience, but the performers as well. His compositions often include indeterminate elements. An indeterminate score gives "the performer a variety of unique ways to play it."[30] Cage's indeterminate scores vary in the number of parameters left to the performer's discretion. Some specify pitch and duration but leave dynamics unspecified, while others, such as *Variations II* (1961), are incredibly flexible. The score of *Variations II* consists "of five small transparencies, each with a single point, and six larger transparencies, each with a single line."[31] These sheets, put on top of one another, create intersecting points and lines. The dots represent notes, while the six lines represent frequency, amplitude, timbre, duration, point of occurrence, and number of notes. Each reading of the transparencies creates a unique event that is interpreted in unique ways, and one can create as many events as one desires. Through his use of indeterminacy, Cage further relinquishes the control traditionally given to a composer. Instead of a static piece of music that allows for very little interpretation, his indeterminate scores act more as tools for creating musical events.

These various actions that Cage implemented are not politically profound *by necessity*. Removing the conductor, for instance, is not liberatory in itself. Just about anyone could do that, and it would not necessarily have any political implications. What makes Cage's actions significant is the challenge—to himself, to the musicians, and to the audience—that he makes these actions entail. By declaring each person an active participant, by placing each person in charge of himself, Cage challenges everyone present to accept the responsibilities incumbent in participating as an equal, rather than just passively observing.

FORMAL STRUCTURE AS SOCIAL SCULPTURE

Cage's music has none of the sloganeering or heavy-handed didacticism one might expect from politically-motivated art. He does not offer music arguing for a political message to be accepted or rejected, but rather offers alternate modes of human interaction existing in actual space and time. He thus attempts to create an oasis in the midst of consumer-driven capitalist society, presenting a society governed by a set of rules entirely different from the dominant culture's. As he noted in a 1991 interview, "If we can have a group in which the individuals are autonomous, then we have a model for society which is free of the need for government, and which could enjoy life."[32]

The society that Cage presents in his work eschews the centralization of power and authority in favor of equal cooperation. As Richard Kostelanetz says of Cage:

> I've always regarded Cage as epitomizing the non-competitive life, where no one is regarded as a threat who must be eliminated, where you can afford to be generous with your own work as well as your possessions, with work so extreme and idiosyncratic that plagiarism need not be feared.[33]

Part of this generosity is demonstrated in his choice of venues. Cage made no elitist distinctions between established concert halls and more grassroots, DIY (Do It Yourself) venues. As Kostelanetz states, Cage "has performed his music in gymnasiums as well as opera houses, the assumption being that all venues are equally legitimate."[34] Cage viewed himself as one among equals, and was willing to collaborate with anyone who wanted, whether that "anyone" was the director of an established concert hall or a motivated individual with an unconventional venue. This equal embrace of venues ties in nicely with Cage's larger contention that his music can act as a form of social modeling. Anyone who wanted to work with him was welcome to do so, and a person's pedigree in the established art world was entirely irrelevant to the equation.

Moreover, if art is to increasingly come under the control of ordinary people, then Cagean works that don't simply *say* how humans could better interact, but actually demonstrate new ways of being, become increasingly useful. If art is to actually impact the community in which it is presented, then bringing people together to experience different types of relationships—stripped of status and privilege—becomes a very useful artistic practice. By facilitating the occurrence of new modes of interaction, Cage demonstrates that different types of relationships are possible. His contentless music supplies a structure in which everyone present, from the composer to the soundman to the audience, can freely place attention in a non-compelled manner. It is quite easy to state that everything would run better without domination or hierarchy, but still another to actually attempt to put it into practice as Cage did.

THE STATE OF ART THEORY

The current, dominant views of art are so far removed from what art ought to be, that the perfectly reasonable views that follow from the works and thoughts of Dewey, Beuys and Cage stand as marginalized, minority viewpoints, rather than common sense accounts of art, creativity and their proper role in human lives and communities. How did we arrive at this state? What has been the trajectory of recent art theory? Why have we reached a point where we must rethink everything and start anew?

Art has been perverted and bastardized by the schism between high art and ordinary life as well as the increasing dominance of the capitalist marketplace. Rather than vital additions to human life, the arts have largely been rendered either hallowed objects with no relation to life as it is lived, or mere commodities and passing fads, as hollow and disposable as any other marketable product. Because the arts have been pushed off their proper course, it is perhaps not surprising that the theory and criticism surrounding the arts has been warped and bastardized as well. As art has been pulled further and further away from its ideal context (human life), the attempts by various thinkers to describe this art have, not surprisingly, been pulled along with it.

THE CREATION OF BEAUTY

In the early eighteenth century, the German philosopher Alexander Gottlieb Baumgarten first used the term "aesthetics" in its modern sense, setting off a series of theories on the nature of art and beauty. Until Baumgarten narrowed the scope of "aesthetics" to sensations of beauty, the term had been used in reference to the study of sensations in general. In his writings on the subject, Baumgarten attempts to establish perceptions of beauty as the sense equivalent of logical deductions. In other words, for Baumgarten, sensations are to beauty as logic is to truth.

There was arguably an historic demand for the development of aesthetics. With the rise of the bourgeoisie, whose private purchase of art created a market beyond the realms of folk art, church-funded religious art, and official portraits of kings, there arose the need for standards of judging good art from bad. In other words, were the bourgeoisie spending wisely? Can "good" art be objectively recognized? Could it be established that when one declares something beautiful, as if beauty were a property of that thing, that this statement is not a mere expression of taste, but a verifiable fact?

In the discussions of art and aesthetics that arose from Baumgarten, two things in particular may strike modern minds as particularly odd. First, natural beauty and artistic beauty are treated as identical, despite the obvious differences between art and nature. Second, there exists an unquestioned assumption that the essence of art is the creation of beauty, a notion later abandoned with the rise of modern art.

Until the publication of Immanuel Kant's *Critique of Judgment*, perhaps the most influential account of aesthetics belongs to David Hume, who, interestingly enough, denies the validity of universal claims of beauty and reduces all aesthetic judgments to taste. In "Of the Standard of Taste," Hume takes the distinctly Humean stance that feelings of beauty are nothing more than expressions of personal preference and can have no objective standards. Human nature is uniform enough that variations in taste are sufficiently minimal to create an appearance of objectivity. But on the occasions when differences in temperament yield differences in taste, the resulting disagreements are irreconcilable.

Kant's additions to the field of aesthetics, while not the final word on the matter, became by far the most influential. The romantics of the nineteenth century latched on to the Kantian notion of the "artist as genius." It was this same notion that Marcel Duchamp mocked and resisted with his readymades in the early twentieth century. Moreover, the modernist focus on form can be traced back to Kant. Given this lasting impact, it will be useful to spend some time unpacking the details of Kant's aesthetics.

KANTIAN AESTHETICS

Summarizing Kant is never an easy task. His later work, the so-called "critical period," consisting of the *Critique of Pure Reason*, the *Critique of Practical Reason*, and the *Critique of Judgment*, constitutes a massive, interlocking system of thought, forcing any of Kant's would-be summarizers to face the related risks of oversimplification and over-explanation. The former leads to a glib overview of a very nuanced system, while the latter leads to an endless exegesis of arcane terminology. So with the caveat that we are about to tread on some dangerous ground, a summary of Kant's aesthetics will begin.

The *Critique of Judgment* cannot be understood without tying it in to Kant's overall metaphysical project, which cannot, in turn, be understood without at least a brief description of the philosophical climate of the eighteenth century, an era dominated by two incommensurable bodies of thought. On one side lies the rationalism exemplified by Gottfried Leibniz, which holds that the world could, and should, be described solely through logical arguments based on *a priori* knowledge—that is, things known independently of experience. On the other side of this philosophical divide stands the empiricism typified by David Hume. Empiricism rejects the existence of *a priori* knowledge and holds that experience is the sole source of everything we know. This schism played itself out along national lines, with the German Leibniz leading his countrymen in the rationalist charge, and Hume bearing the empiricist standard in front of a host of British thinkers. This same schism carried over into aesthetics. Recall that the German Baumgarten declared judgments of taste akin to logic—the ultimate example of innate, *a priori* knowledge in the rationalist arsenal—while Hume reduced beauty to experience-based taste.

Kant attempted to act as a sort of referee between these diametrically opposed schools of thought, both in metaphysics and aesthetics. Kant devised the notion of the *synthetic a priori*, which refers to ideas derived (or synthesized) from experience, but provable with *a priori* knowledge. The clearest examples of what Kant had in mind are geometric. For instance, by applying an *a priori* understanding of space with an empirical investigation of triangles, it can be determined that the sum of any triangle's angles will equal 180°. If one finds a triangle whose angles equal a different sum, this is not an example of experience disproving geometry, but simply a math error. The fact that a triangle's angles will total 180° is an example of *synthetic a priori* knowledge. For Kant, everything we really know is derived by filtering the empirical through the innate. We receive sense data and process it through our inborn systems. But the source of this sense data, the world as it is in itself, remains forever beyond our grasp. All we can ever know is sense data, and the only way we can process it is through our given modes of understanding. We can neither move beyond sense data, nor our ways of processing it. It is also important to note that, for Kant, these innate systems of understanding are identical in all humans, as this universality is a key component in his account of aesthetic judgments as objectively verifiable.

In the *Critique of Judgment*, Kant attempts to show that judgments of beauty, though seemingly subjective, can be examples of *synthetic a priori* knowledge. Though gathered through experience, properly executed aesthetic judgments are tied to our innate systems in such a way that no experience could disprove them. But how is this possible? How can Kant reasonably claim that aesthetic judgments can be universal, necessary, and irrefutable? According to Kant, this is possible if aesthetic judgments are made disinterestedly, thus avoiding the pitfalls of charm and emotion. By removing personal dispositions from the equation, one helps ensure that the judgment is universal. One may still derive a feeling of personal pleasure from viewing an aesthetically enjoyable object, but this ought to result from a disinterested appreciation of its form, rather than from one's desires or personal preferences. Moreover, an appreciated object should be viewed as having no apparent purpose. It should be seen as a final product with no reference to the rest of the world, and no function beyond merely being. A functional object, such as a vase, may still be beautiful, but only if it is judged on formal criteria, and not as a useful thing.

Kant would further have one ignore elements that he interprets as entirely sense-bound, such as color and tone, as these are too personal and too disconnected from our innate systems. Form is the only basis of indisputable beauty, as judgments based on form are tied to our innate understanding of space and time. This is where the *Critique of Judgment* becomes linked to Kant's larger metaphysical project. By connecting aesthetic judgments to our *a priori*, innate, and most importantly, *universal* understanding of space and time, these judgments likewise become universal. Joined to basic human cognition, but stripped of the personal, aesthetic judgments become verifiable by *any* human's cognition.

Kant applies his account of aesthetic judgment equally to art and nature. This may seem strange, as nature lends itself more easily to disinterested appreciation, while art, having been presumably created with a purpose and personal elements, would be unfairly reduced to form at the expense of these other important factors. But Kant argues that art ought to be judged in the same disinterested way as nature, even though one is fully aware of the "artificial" creative process behind art. According to Kant, when we judge art, we must forget that someone made it, and take it in as pure form with no apparent purpose or utility.

So this is how Kant feels art ought to be appreciated, but how does art get made in the first place? It is actually refreshing that Kant even addresses this topic. Previous aestheticians, like Baumgarten and Hume, focus on judging finished objects, while entirely ignoring how those things got there in the first place. But Kant has a model for the act of creation. He claims that the formula for fine art is genius tempered by taste. Genius is a talent for producing that for which no rule can be given. The creation of art cannot be taught. Certainly, techniques for drawing or sculpting can be taught, but the inception of a true work of genius cannot. To Kant, an artist possesses the unexplainable ability to conjure new ideas out of thin air, a skill not even the artist understands. But ideas of genius still need to be tempered by the same disinterested good taste that recognizes beauty.

MODERNISM AND THE DEVELOPMENT OF FORM

Kant's claims constitute a view of art entirely unlike Dewey's. While Dewey sees art as arising directly from experience, addressing that experience, and only understandable within the context of that experience, Kant sees the perception of beauty and the application of good taste as linked to our *a priori* understandings of space and time and separate from particular, unique experiences. Notably, Joseph Beuys also resisted a focus on form. As he stated,

> After all, we live in a culture that regards art in formal terms and repeatedly says that fine arts are retinal, are just grasped by the eye. [...] But if that's all that's happening, then, no interesting painting can come about, it will just decline into surface form.[35]

John Cage, in a seemingly Kantian move, sought to create works that were only form with no content. Yet, despite this contentlessness, his works still point toward life and experience. *4'33"*, the silent piece, leaves nothing to listen to but the world. As such, it radically situates the listener within corporeal day-to-day experience, creating continuity between aesthetic experiences and ordinary processes of living. Moreover, by using music as a means of changing minds, Cage sought to impact our understanding and experience of the world. Despite his focus on form, Cage has much more in common with Dewey and Beuys than Kant.

It was not until the rise of Modernism that Kantian aesthetics were eclipsed as the dominant theory of art, though some Kantian elements were carried over into modernism.

Modernism did away with the assumption that art is the creation of beauty, but maintained Kant's focus on form. Rather than describe art as a fairly static series of stabs at beauty—a notion of beauty linked to innate, universal, and unchanging *a priori* notions of space and time—the modernists focused on the *history* of art and the *development* of form. According to the modernists, art progresses through a series of formal developments following one another logically and linearly. With modernism, form remains as central as it was for Kant, but its role changes dramatically.

Modernism, and eventually, postmodernism have been the dominant theories of the arts and culture since the late nineteenth century. Postmodernism arose from, and in reaction to, modernism in the late twentieth century, supplanting its supremacy. Both schools of thought presuppose a separation between art and life. In modernism in particular, art is viewed not as an integral element in day-to-day human life, but as a separate entity with laws and a logic of its own that artists essentially "step in to" and help along. The modernist creation of a very peculiar, very artificial account of progress, and the postmodernist rejection of that same peculiar progress provides a particularly tidy point of contention between these schools of thought that furnishes a framework for a more orderly summary.

The modernist account of art is marked by the belief that art history has a narrative with a quasi-teleological thrust. To the modernist, art *progresses*. Not coincidentally, one of the defining features of postmodernism—that which makes it so *post* modernism—is its rejection of progress. This rejection occurs for a number of often overlapping reasons that will be discussed below. But unfortunately for anyone rooting for the long-term viability of postmodernism as a body of thought, modernism's version of progress is inherently problematic to begin with, thereby rendering postmodernism's rejection of that same progress equally problematic.

Clement Greenberg and Theodor Adorno put forward two of the most recognized and influential accounts of modernism in the arts. Although Greenberg focused on visual art while Adorno focused on music and literature, similarities exist between their respective accounts of modernism, in particular in their focus on progress in the arts. As Andreas Huyssen writes in *After The Great Divide*:

> While there are major differences between the two men, both in temperament and in the scope of their analyses, they both share a notion of the inevitability of the evolution of modern art. To put it bluntly, they believe in progress—if not in society, then certainly in art.[36]

And it is this modernist belief in artistic progress that represents one of the main divergences between the modern and the postmodern.

Those who would place us in the postmodern era declare the modernist notion of progress useless for several reasons. Some reject the "master narratives" of modernism espoused by the likes of Greenberg and Adorno as elitist and Eurocentric. Greenberg drew a line of constant innovation from Manet to the New York school of abstract expressionism. Adorno saw Beethoven starting a procession of progression leading directly to Schoenberg's serialism. In either case, the view is that great men create great art that transcends mass culture and moves forever forward into ever greater feats of innovation. Postmodernists who criticize this version of progress as elitist or Eurocentric are correct in their criticism. The postmodernist Frederic Jameson speaks of the "prophetic elitism and authoritarianism of the modern movement."[37] Greenberg and Adorno's belief that art history can be effectively discussed while focusing solely on formal developments in western culture as practiced by a handful of individuals, while simultaneously ignoring the activities of the rest of the globe or anyone else who does not serve their narrative, is both a smug oversimplification and frighteningly elitist. In short, the modernist account of art history and the nature of progress is inherently problematic. But it is by no means the only imaginable version of progress. It is but one possible version, and a pretty poor one at that. Postmodernists who use this flawed account of progress in order to either declare the narrative of art history complete, to declare progress now impossible, or even to reject the very notion of progress, base their entire discussion on a very questionable definition of the word "progress."

Moreover, postmodernists all too quickly accept the modernist contention that the great modern artists were able to stand outside of the capitalist marketplace with their work, thereby maintaining a kind of purity that allowed them the luxury to experiment and progress. This was apparently due to their art being "high" rather than "low." But in the postmodern era, this distinction is declared gone. The space between high and low has collapsed. Therefore, it is concluded, it is now impossible to create work outside of the capitalist marketplace or with the same level of purity as modern artists. But, as will be shown later, the modernist claim to have ever stood outside of the marketplace is highly questionable. In fact, it was not until the advent of the free market that artists were able to free themselves from the church and the state and survive off of art created, well, for the free market. It was the rise of the bourgeoisie as high art's target market that gave modern artists the luxury to experiment. In reality, an artist's ability to transcend the marketplace is due to factors that have nothing to do with the often quite specious high/low distinction.

Since the modernist claims about progress in the arts are mistaken, the postmodernist counterclaims that progress has either reached its end or has been rendered impossible must be abandoned. The modernists got progress wrong to begin with, and the postmodernists adopted these errors as their own. But the modernist version is not the only possible form of progress. The concept can be reframed to be more inclusive and less reductive. But before this new version of progress can be discussed, we must confront with the thorny business of modernism, postmodernism, and the death of progress. Its resurrection will come later.

KITSCH AND CONSERVATISM

Clement Greenberg provided the prosecution with plenty of evidence for the case of modernism's elitism. In his 1939 essay "Avant-Garde and Kitsch," he blames the rise in literacy for the debasement of art. Allowing commoners and riff-raff the knowledge needed to take in cultural commodities sullied and desecrated art's good name by providing kitsch with an audience. Greenberg defines kitsch as "popular, commercial art and literature with their chromeotypes, magazine covers, illustrations, ads, slick and pulp fiction, comics, Tin Pan Alley music, tap dancing, Hollywood movies etc., etc."[38] He further elaborates: "Kitsch is vicarious experience and faked sensations, kitsch changes according to style, but remains the same. Kitsch is the epitome of all that is spurious in the life of our times."[39]

Avant-Garde art, of which modernism is an example,[40] is a representative of "true culture." Greenberg dates the beginning of modern art to 1850s France with Baudelaire in literature and Manet in painting. He claims that as the masses began devouring mass-produced culture, aesthetic standards declined. Because of this, artists were forced to push forward (and progress) in order to maintain these slipping aesthetic standards. To quote Greenberg: "So I come at last to what I offer as an embracing and perdurable definition of Modernism: that it consists in the continuing endeavor to stem the decline of aesthetic standards threatened by the relative democratization of culture under industrialism; that the overriding and innermost logic of Modernism is to maintain the levels of the past in the face of an opposition that hadn't been present in the past."[41]

Thus, Greenberg places the notion of progress central to modernism, strangely enough, in a form of conservatism, in a need to maintain high art's high standards against the unwashed masses pounding at the gates of culture, comic books in hand. In order to stay ahead of the democratization and debasement of culture, it proved necessary to push forward with art's historically necessary formal innovations at an accelerated pace. As he writes, "over the past hundred and thirty years and more the best new painting and sculpture (and the best new poetry) have in their time proven a challenge and a trial to the art lover—a challenge and a trial as they hadn't been used to."[42] In other words, because of the modern artist's need to arrive at new formal innovations quickly in order to stay ahead of culture's debasement, audiences were often left perplexed. But, he points out, "with only a relatively small lapse of time the innovations of modernism begin to look less and less radical, and [...] they almost settle into place eventually as part of the continuum of high Western art along with Shakespeare's verse and Rembrandt's drawings."[43] That is, these once perplexing formal innovations were simply those that would have occurred anyway as artists followed the logic of art history, but due to the accelerated pace at which these innovations occurred, it took some time before audiences were ready to understand them as a natural part of art's trajectory.

Greenberg's account of progress requires a distinction between art and life. Art is depicted as an entity unto itself with a life of its own. By Greenberg's reckoning, an artist steps into a separate realm that is "art" and makes the works demanded by the logic of that realm and *its* natural progression, rather than the logic and natural progression of the *artist's* life and experience.

THE END OF ART

Arthur Danto, in *Beyond the Brillo Box*, accepts the general modernist notion that art history has a narrative, that is, that it *progresses*. But Danto claims that this narrative has drawn to a close. Art has reached its end. There can be no more formal innovations. There can only be the art produced after the end of art. Danto places this terminus, somewhat arbitrarily, with Andy Warhol's *Brillo Boxes* of 1965. These were plywood boxes screened with an exact reproduction of the actual Brillo boxes in which one might find an actual Brillo pad.

So thanks to these *Brillo Boxes*, art history has drawn to a close. But, Danto writes, "What the end of art means is not, of course, that there will be no more works of art." He explains: "What has come to an end, rather, is a certain narrative, under the terms of which making art was understood to be carrying forward the history of discovery and making breakthroughs."[44] Danto accepts the basic tenets of modernist art criticism as exemplified by someone like Clement Greenberg. At the very least, we can probably safely impute to Danto Greenberg's notion that art has—or rather, had—a narrative. It moves forward through a process of experiment, discovery, and formal breakthrough. Important work is that which is historically necessary for the continuation of the narrative. But Danto declares the process complete. Art has reached its end.

To better explain his contention, Danto refers back to an 1828 lecture Hegel delivered concerning the philosophy of art. Hegel held that art would reach an historical end and turn into something else, namely, philosophy. All artistic changes and innovations, Hegel claimed, are simply art trying to define itself, to mark out its own boundaries. But once art has determined its boundaries—that is, once the exact nature of art has become known—then art can no longer have a history because it cannot develop any further. All that can be made is art about the nature of art.

This, Danto argues, is exactly what occurred on that fateful day in 1965 when Andy Warhol displayed his *Brillo Boxes* and effectively ended art history. All an artist can do now is dabble in styles from the past. As Danto writes, "One can in truth be an avant-garde artist, but, unlike Dada in 1919, this is now just a style rather than a historical moment."[45]

But should anyone even accept the modernist version of art history? It is riddled with difficulties and troublesome generalizations. For instance, it is dreadfully reductive and exclusionary in its quest to tell a single story about the history of art. The modernist account of painting, for example, focuses on a movement toward a two-dimensional picture plane that does nothing to hide its two-dimensionality. In the Renaissance, artists applied blobs of colored pigments to canvas in such a way that the blobs of pigment resembled three-dimensional space. But with modernism, Manet and his ilk began applying blobs of pigment in such a way that, although an object from the world was still represented, it was clear to everyone that the painting was, well, a painting. As the modern era progressed, representation receded even further into the background and paint began to be applied in such a way that a finished painting was eventually just a canvas with paint on it, and not a picture of anything at all. The paint was simply paint, and the canvas did not try to fool anyone into thinking it had any more dimensions than it actually did. This reached its apotheosis (according to Clement Greenberg) with abstract expressionism. Greenberg describes his conception of the history of painting in his essay "Abstract, Representational, and So Forth":

From Giotto to Courbet, the painter's first task had been to hollow out an illusion of three-dimensional space on a flat surface. One looked through this surface as through a proscenium onto a stage. Modernism has rendered this stage shallower and shallower until now its backdrop has become the same as its curtain, which has now become all that the painter has left to work on. [...] The picture has now become an entity belonging to the same order of space as our bodies; it is no longer the vehicle of an imagined equivalent of that order. Pictorial space has lost its "inside" and become all "outside." The spectator can no longer escape into it from the space in which he himself stands.[46]

This narrative is very orderly. But why should the history of art be orderly? This narrative pushes off to the perimeter anyone who does not fit into its tidy boundaries. Were you focused on the two-dimensionality of the picture plane? No? Well, that's too bad. You'll be relegated to a footnote. What about you? Are you from the West? No? You're from Asia? I'm sorry. Your art just isn't part of the history of art. We'll have to put it in the "World" section of our textbook.

Anything that reduces the history of a phenomenon as complex and varied as all of humanity's paintings from the Renaissance through the 1950s to a single narrative with a single goal ought to be distrusted. Actually, more than distrusted, it should be thrown out as an absurdity. Such reductive, teleological narratives invariably force a wealth of information into neat, tidy boundaries while ignoring the true complexity of the subject under discussion. But this absurd narrative is exactly what Danto uses as his basic framework. *Beyond the Brillo Box* is loaded with fascinating passages and beautifully constructed arguments. The problem lies in the fact that all of these fascinating passages and beautiful arguments are based on an inherently flawed narrative of art history. Danto accepts the shaky premises of the modernists, brings these shaky premises to an equally shaky conclusion, and then throws up his hands because he has run out of ideas. Near the end of his introduction to *Beyond the Brillo Box*, he writes, "the master narrative of Western art is losing its grip and nothing has taken its place. My thought is that nothing can."[47] This displays a troubling lack of imagination on the part of a writer as talented as Danto. Art history does not require a master narrative. It has thousands upon thousands of interlinking and interconnected narratives. It is simply too rich and complex to have a single teleological thrust.

ART AND HISTORICAL CONTEXT

Danto constantly stresses the importance of understanding a work's historical context in order to fully understand it as art. As he writes, "to interpret a work is to be committed to a historical explanation of the work."[48] Danto is correct. We require extensive archeological, anthropological and art historical explanations in order to make sense (for instance) of the cave paintings of Lascaux. Such was not the case for the inhabitants of Lascaux when the works were created. For them, the cave paintings spoke to the questions and concerns of their own historical milieu. Similarly, Warhol's works embodied meanings that "belonged to the common culture of the time." His subject matter was "instantly recognizable to whoever lived the life of the common culture. The art redeemed the signs that meant enormously much to everyone, as defining their daily lives. Warmth, nourishment, orderliness, and predictability are profound human values which the stacked cans of Campbell's soup exemplify."[49] Centuries from now, Warhol's works, much like the Lascaux caves, will require anthropological and art historical explanations in order to be fully appreciated. Danto is correct that what makes one object art and another object not art is historically determined.[50] A blank canvas in the 1860s was just a blank canvas. By the 1960s, a blank canvas could be hung in a gallery and make a profound statement about the nature of art. Danto's mistake is taking the fact that each individual artwork's meaning is historically determined, and often historically determined by its relationship to other works in the history of art, to further impute that art *as a whole* has a single narrative that follows a logical path to a single terminus. Although art changes over time, and although many works are historically connected, this does not imply that there is one single thread running through all of art history.

Danto's overall contention that there can be no more formal innovations in art, only genre exercises that refer back to the bygone days of genres, complicates his contention that art's meaning is historically dependent. These two contentions together imply that the future cultural context for artworks, objects that will mean "enormously much to everyone, as defining their daily lives," will be adequately served by mere dabblings in art historical styles from other historical contexts. In other words, if Danto's prediction about *art's* future is true, then the future in which this art will be created will be a very gray, dull place indeed. There will be nothing new under the sun, just old ideas rehashed. And this will somehow be sufficient. Danto apparently holds the artists of the future in very low regard, as he assumes that they will not be able to speak to the new concerns of their age in new ways. Only hollow genre exercises will be possible.

CHAPTER 6

POSTMODERNISM AND THE POSSIBILITY OF DISSENT

We are living in the era after the *Brillo Boxes*. Besides art having reached its supposed terminus, the modernist distinction between high art and mass culture has been erased. The images on the Brillo Boxes in the grocery store are the same as the ones in the museum. The form and content of high art and low art are now identical.

This distinction (between high and low) is a specifically modernist one. Clement Greenberg drew a line between avant-garde and kitsch. Theodor Adorno made a similar distinction between high art and mass culture (that will be discussed below). This modernist distinction, though based on questionable premises, became a basic presupposition in postmodern thought, feeding into the distinctly postmodern claim that cultural resistance has been rendered impossible by the fall of high art into the marketplace (or the ascendance of the marketplace into high art).

It is true that there *is* a distinction between high and low art. A garage band playing the same three chords for an hour is noticeably different from an orchestra performing Mozart. Where the modernists erred was in supposing that an unbridgeable chasm exists between high and low. There *is* a difference. Hence the distinction made throughout this book between the *different* ways in which museumified high art and the products of the culture industry have separated art from life. However, the distinction between high and low is a fluid one, and the majority of the world's artworks do not fall easily into either extreme. In reality, the distinction operates on a sliding scale with no rigid lines of demarcation. There are no actual characteristics, formal or otherwise, firmly separating high art from low. Formal tricks and bits of content are borrowed and shared from one end of the spectrum of art to the other. Moreover, this borrowing occurs in both directions—from high to low and low to high—and most importantly, this borrowing is by no means a new development or unique to the postmodern era.

AFTER MODERNISM AND MASS CULTURE

Theodor Adorno was a member of the Frankfurt School, a group of like-minded thinkers who came together at the Institute for Social Research at the University of Frankfurt in the 1930s. This group included, among others, Max Horkheimer and Herbert Marcuse. Adorno viewed "mass culture," basically synonymous with Greenberg's kitsch, as a means for mollifying the masses and fostering docility by providing readily-available, but mindless, cultural products. In his essay "Perennial Fashion—Jazz," Adorno discusses and dismisses jazz as exactly this sort of mindless mass culture.

> The ban on changing the basic beat during the course of the music is itself sufficient to constrict composition to the point where what it demands is not aesthetic awareness of style but rather psychological regression. The limitations placed on metre, harmony and form are no less stifling. Considered as a whole, the perennial sameness of jazz consists not in a basic organization of the material in which the imagination can roam freely and without inhibition, as within an articulate language, but rather in the utilization of certain well-defined tricks, formulas and clichés to the exclusion of everything else.[51]

Adorno then turns to what this lack of formal freedom says about the possibility of cultural criticism through mass culture.

> The more totally the culture industry roots out all deviations, thus cutting the medium off from its intrinsic possibilities of development, the more the whole blaring dynamic business reaches a standstill. Just as no piece of jazz can, in a musical sense, be said to have a history, just as all its components can be moved about at will, just as no single measure follows from the logic of the musical progression—so the perennial fashion becomes a likeness of a planned congealed society, not so different from the nightmare vision of Huxley's *Brave New World*.[52]

In Adorno's conception, high art, of which modern art is an example, is not prey to the same weaknesses as mass culture. It is not tied to business and does not need to satisfy popular tastes. It is therefore free to progress by its own logic.

This basic distinction between high and low developed by modernists like Greenberg and Adorno has been taken up by postmodern thinkers and used to demonstrate the ways in which cultural resistance has been rendered futile in the postmodern age. The "whole blaring dynamic business has reached a standstill." Not only is progress is impossible, but all art has been subsumed by the massive being of world capitalism, and as such, no art is in any position to mount any kind of critique on the prevailing economic order. In a particularly bleak passage in his exceptionally bleak *Postmodernism, or, The Cultural Logic of Late Capitalism*, Frederic Jameson states:

> No theory of cultural politics current on the Left today has been able to do without one notion or another of a certain minimal aesthetic distance, of the possibility of positioning the cultural act outside the massive Being of capital, from which to assault this last. What the burden of our preceding demonstration suggests, however, is that distance in general (including "critical distance" in particular) has very precisely been abolished in the new space of postmodernism.[53]

This ties in to his point that a fundamental feature of modernism was a "hostility to the market itself," and that this hostility has been inverted into an embrace in the postmodern era.[54] Modernists like Adorno believed in a distinction between high art and mass culture, and felt that it was possible for high art to stand apart from the mass market and comment from outside. But now, Jameson claims, high has become low and low has become high. All that exists is the market, and the only place where anything can ever happen is the marketplace. The "minimal aesthetic distance" required for criticism is gone.

There are several problems here. First, Jameson readily succumbs to a fatalistic form of historical determinism that leaves no room for human agency. There is no compelling reason ever given as to *why* the historical circumstances of the postmodern era are so all-encompassing that literally *no one* is in a position to step outside the marketplace and create a non-commodifiable work or comment upon commodity culture. But more importantly, Jameson all-too-readily accepts the modernist stance that high art is the only realm in which non-commodifiable arts and acts can be made. Having accepted this questionable initial premise, Jameson concludes that the collapse of the high/low distinction has made it impossible for art to be anything other than just another feature of market capitalism. And with this comes a loss of "critical distance" and progress in the arts, as any imaginable act will always be subsumed under the "massive Being of capital," thus leaving the arts stalled in place, bent to the mighty will of the market.

There are, again, mistaken assumptions in the modernist beliefs about art and progress, as well as the conditions required for cultural dissent. And it is these mistaken assumptions that postmodernist commentators invariably use in their rejection of the possibility of both artistic progress and cultural dissent.

Jameson accepts Adorno and Greenberg's distinction between mass culture and modernism as historically accurate. He echoes Greenberg's claim that modernism was a reaction to the rise of mass culture when he writes that modernism's function consisted "at least in part in the securing of a realm of authentic experience over the surrounding environment of middle- and low-brow culture. Indeed it can be argued that the emergence of high modernism is itself contemporaneous with the first great expansion of a recognizably mass culture."[55] And having accepted this questionable modernist premise, Jameson then turns around and applies it to his equally questionable postmodernist arguments regarding the possibility of cultural resistance.

THE HIGH / LOW DIVIDE

Both the modernists and postmodernists observe the simultaneous rise of modern art and mass culture in the mid-nineteenth century and posit the former to be a reaction to the latter. Just as simple an explanation and more likely the case is this: modern art and mass culture arose nearly contemporaneously due to the advent of industrial capitalism. A new class, the bourgeoisie, arose with the money to spend on expensive cultural commodities, thus creating an art market independent of the church or the state, thereby allowing artists to create works of their own choosing and place them in the marketplace. At the same time, a growing mass of urban workers emerged who created a demand for mass culture and popular entertainment. Both new classes thus created new demands for new cultural products.

Jameson claims that the distinction between modernism and mass culture "no longer seems functional,"[56] but it is questionable whether or not it was ever accurate in the first place. The distinction was never as tidy and simple as Jameson, Adorno, and Greenberg suppose. There is a sliding scale for an artwork's highness or lowness that existed long before postmodernism. There is no clear, unambiguous formal element that can render a work high or low. Even Greenberg admits as much when he states that "Kitsch is deceptive. It has many different levels, and some of them are high enough to be dangerous to the naïve seeker of true light."[57] He also speaks of "puzzling borderline cases" like the novelists "Simenon, in France, and Steinbeck in this country."[58]

Pablo Picasso, whose membership in the modernist canon cannot be disputed, regularly utilized imagery from the supposedly "low" and "primitive" art of African tribal masks in his work near the beginning of the twentieth century. "He was convinced not only that the art of his childhood—along with the religious, ethical, and sexual beliefs embodied in it—was no longer viable, but that it was incumbent on him to provide new alternatives."[59] At the Musée d'Ethnographie du Trocadéro, he witnessed an exhibition of African art. "'At that moment,' he said later, 'I realized what painting was all about.'"[60] This was not a simple case of Picasso "quoting" these works. He felt that there were images and values in African art worth appropriating into his own life and art. Modern art, at a fairly early stage, and in the person of one of its key figures, thus crossed the great divide between high and low, or in this case, between high art and folk art, in a complex way that calls into question the modernist supposition of a distinct line of demarcation between high and low.

Bernard Gendron, in *Popular Music and the Avant-Garde: Between Montmartre and the Mudd Club*, makes a strong case that the dividing line between high and low culture was not first crossed in the postmodern era, nor was all the borrowing a case of mass culture appropriating high art's innovations. He writes that "We need only recall the Jazz Age of the 1920s when the avant-gardes of Paris and Berlin were enthusiastically consuming jazz and attempting to assimilate its aesthetic into their own practices,"[61] or the cabarets of mid nineteenth century France that presented high and low art on the same stage and often combined these two supposedly separate fields of cultural practice.[62] Because of these often ignored, but impossible to deny, exchanges between high and low, Gendron declares "the original postmodern theory of high/low" as "altogether in tatters."[63]

CAPITAL AND CULTURAL RESISTANCE

But Jameson holds to this tattered, questionable distinction in spite of its dubious veracity. He uses the loss of the probably-never-existent high/low distinction as proof that art has lost its ability to stand outside the marketplace. Both the modernists and postmodernists have based their beliefs about high art, low art, and the possibility of firing an artistically-based sortie against the prevailing order on a series of falsely-drawn generalizations that in no way describe the complexity and fluidity inherent in the relationship between various realms of artistic practice. Greenberg and Adorno put an absolute divide between actually overlapping artistic activities. Jameson then takes this artificial divide and uses it to draw a similarly artificial conclusion about the possibility of progress and cultural resistance.

Because these suppositions regarding the possibility of cultural resistance and artistic progress are mistaken, it is worth reevaluating the political possibilities of the arts. Jameson declares that every element of life has been subsumed by the capitalist marketplace and that there is no escape from this situation. All dissent will inevitably be commodified, turning resistance into just another fashion that can fatten corporate pockets.

Jameson is only partially correct. He errs in decreeing cultural dissent an absolute impossibility. Granted, creating a realm for artistic practice beyond the confines of the marketplace is indeed a difficult proposition. It will involve completely rethinking the role and function of the arts. Cultural institutions that operate on a human scale and create art divorced from business motives will need to exist.

A key facet in creating these proposed institutions involves a reimagining of artistic progress—a version based on progress as experienced in the natural world. This version of artistic progress would embrace increased individuation and subjectivity, and would simultaneously seek means of resisting commodification by creating works that would only fully function on a human scale, as essential elements in thriving, decentralized communities.

THE ECOLOGY OF ART

The debate about the possibility of progress needs to be reframed. Modernist assumptions are flawed, and postmodernist rejections of progress are based on these same flawed assumptions. Progress need not be authoritarian, elitist, or focused on one small thread of western culture. High art is not the only means for taking an artistic stand outside of commodity culture (and it never really was).

Progress should be redefined in ecological terms. The bifurcation of the world into many distinct narratives (a bifurcation that the postmodernists bemoan as a loss of "master narratives" and progress) is potentially a form of progress in itself. The modernist account of artistic progress utilizes a centralized story in which all artistic activity is organized around a single narrative. But the arts can only truly thrive when individuation, complexity, and subjectivity are maximized. Humanity's artistic needs cannot be met by a simplified and centralized art world, but rather, only by a complex art world driven by countless unique narratives, interlinked in complex ways.

In ecology, monocultures are unhealthy ecosystems. In the natural world, the healthiest and most advanced ecosystems are those teeming with different organisms leading separate but interrelated lives. As Murray Bookchin writes in *The Ecology of Freedom*, "Farmers have repeatedly met with disastrous results because of the conventional emphasis on single-crop approaches to agriculture or *monoculture*, to use a widely accepted term for those endless wheat and corn fields that extend to the horizon in many parts of the world. Without the mixed crops that normally provide both the countervailing forces and mutualistic support that come with mixed populations of plants and animals, the entire agricultural situation in an area has been known to collapse."[64]

Artistic progress should be understood in the same terms as progress in the natural world. There is not one single goal toward which nature, when healthy, heads. Instead, there are thousands upon thousands of interlinked goals all occurring simultaneously. Similarly, true artistic progress comes from thousands upon thousands of artistic narratives interlinking and interacting. Our current, highly reductive understanding of art leads to a critical search for *the* important work, or *the* important artist in any given period. To reduce a period of art to some "really important work" would be like talking about a "really important, epoch-defining sandwich"[65] someone made, or a "really important, truly groundbreaking parking space" someone found, or a "really important sunburn" someone developed that captured not just UV rays, but the zeitgeist as well.

When functioning well, art, like nature, is a complex mess of various activities. This embrace of complexity is not a call for chaos. In fact, there could be greater unity through such variety, as the greater variety creates a richer and more complex whole. As Bookchin says of natural complexity, in a statement that could just as easily be applied to the arts, "ecological wholeness is not an immutable homogeneity but rather the very opposite—a dynamic *unity of diversity*. In nature, balance and harmony are achieved by ever-changing differentiation, by ever-expanding diversity."[66] And such a rich and complex whole, in both nature and the arts, can only be the end result of progress.

Art should be recreated to approximate an ecosystem that grows, changes, and evolves, but not in a neat, orderly way. Rather, there ought to be a tangled mess of interactions and symbiotic relationships that change over time, leading to growth, adaptation, and yes, progress. We ought to utilize a wide variety of artistic practices and activities in order to arrive at a richer, more meaningful art world with ever increasing complexity, subjectivity, and individuation. Progress is not linear or teleological in the natural world *or* the art world.

NATURE AND IDEOLOGY

It should be clear that a diversified ecosystem is far more stable, far less prone to collapse, and far preferable to the monocultures sown by the factory farms of industrial capitalism. So why are these monocultures allowed to exist at all, let alone to dominate our land? The answer to this question brings to the foreground ideological assumptions common to capitalism. Bringing these (often) hidden ideological assumptions into focus not only exposes the roots of some of our current views of the natural world, but simultaneously uncovers eerily similar ideological undercurrents informing our current views of art.

Capitalism is not unique in foisting its ideology onto nature.[67] The dominant ideology of any given period is almost invariably reflected in its understanding of the natural world. Many tribal communities, organized into clans, saw nature itself as similarly organized into clans. Medieval society, with a hierarchical organization from serfs to kings, saw nature organized hierarchically, and sought a king of the jungle. Capitalist society, with its grow-or-die mentality, and eat-or-be-eaten philosophy, imputes the same level of competition endemic to the marketplace onto the natural world, which is portrayed as composed of preys and predators, competing within and across species for limited resources. Despite claims to the contrary, this particular view was not a necessary corollary to the advent of Darwinism. Cooperation and symbiosis are just as important in evolution, if not more important, than competition and survival of the fittest.

Similarly, just as capitalism reduces all entities to saleable commodities, nature is viewed as just another item to buy, sell, and trade in the marketplace. Owing to the capitalist drive for endless expansion, nature has been warped out of shape. In an endless pursuit of more, more, and more, never-ending monocultural rows have been laid over leveled hills, leeching the soil of all the nutrients it once held. Like previous ideologies, the values of capitalism are reflected in contemporaneous views of the natural world. But unlike these previous ideologies, capitalism does far more than simply foster a special ideolological *understanding* of nature. It also fosters its destruction. Just as humans move through a series of market-based, inherently antagonistic relationships with one another—each playing buyer and seller in turn, each trying to buy low and sell high—nature has also become just another antagonistic partner in the dance of commerce. Just as humans are made isolated monads by capitalism—severed from the mutually beneficial consociations that life ought to entail—nature has also been rendered separate from each and every human, just another "other" that can supply the means to a profitable ends.

These distinctly capitalist, and decidedly destructive views—that nature is as competitive as the marketplace and ought to supply that marketplace with everything it demands and more—are also reflected in modernist and postmodernist views of artistic progress. Movements develop new formal traits, thereby defeating and replacing previous movements. A series of different artists are declared the new great, and the winner's vanquished prey becomes lost to history. Just as capitalism reduces complex ecosystems to monocultures, so too does the reductive and simplified view of art endemic to capitalism insist upon a single line of progress snaking through time—a monoculture of a different sort. Further, just as capitalism treats the natural world as a source of exploitable resources, so that any piece of land may be reduced to nothing more than a source of profit, monetary value is equally made central to art. The arts section of most major newspapers spend as much time discussing new records at art auctions as they do discussing art's value *as art*. Monetary worth, rather than artistic worth, has become the most notable aspect of art. Art has become just another commodity, subsumed by the market. Postmodernists are correct in noting this. Where they err is assuming that there is no escape from this situation.

ART AND PROGRESS

Our ideological assumptions need to be recognized and removed. By replacing these assumptions with new views of what art, nature, and society are capable, we take a collective step toward the creative reshaping of our world. By redefining progress in ecological terms, reintroducing human agency, democratizing, and decentralizing the production and consumption of art, we see that progress can still exist in the arts, not through a single movement towards a single goal, but through the creation of a rich and complex whole. Ultimately, the postmodern rejection of progress is just as mistaken as the modernist acceptance of it. If progress is defined as the flattening of the picture plane or the inclusion of more and more atonality in music, then artistic progress does little good for anyone. But if artistic progress is defined as an increasing decentralization of art in general, a democratization of high art, and a movement towards more community involvement around the creation and distribution of works of art, then artistic progress will become a useful notion for individuals beyond art history professors who require a neat, orderly notion of art history to structure their lectures around.

CHAPTER 8

DIY AND THE FUTURE OF COMMUNITY

There have been numerous artistic activities conducted in the last several decades that *have* sought to democratize the production and consumption of culture and place it in human hands on a human scale. One of the best examples is DIY (Do It Yourself) culture, which is most closely associated with underground punk rock, though its ethos and tactics have been appropriated by numerous different fields, from craft fairs to the visual arts. DIY culture is exactly what it sounds like. Artists literally do it themselves, taking the means of cultural production into their own hands—creating small artist-run record labels, fanzines, music venues, and art galleries—all outside the confines of the culture industry, allowing artists with works deemed unmarketable by the mainstream to disseminate their art on their own terms without being forced to sanitize or degrade it. There are limits to the political efficacy of DIY culture, but before discussing these limitations, it is worth delving into some of the lofty and often inspirational goals inherent to it.

What was the genesis of DIY culture? The majority of the earliest and most well-known punk acts, such as the Sex Pistols, The Clash, and The Ramones, all had albums released by large, established labels. Their sound may have been more aggressive and dissonant than most of what was available in the 1970s, but the system that presented them was the same one that presented everything else. It was more of the same thing, just dressed in new costumes. Penny Rimbaud, the drummer for hardcore punk act Crass, claims that he was initially excited by these mainstream punk acts. He writes, "The Pistols, The Damned, The Clash: new sounds, new vocabulary."[68] But, "Within six months the movement had been bought out. The capitalist counter-revolutionaries had killed with cash. Punk degenerated from being a force for change, to becoming just another element in the grand media circus. Sold out, sanitized and strangled, punk had become just another social commodity, a burnt-out memory of how it might have been."[69]

Eventually, however, even more aggressive and less popularly palatable acts arose, and many of these, whether by choice or necessity, embraced a DIY ethos eschewing the grand media circus Penny Rimbaud found so distasteful. Minor Threat in the United States and Crass in the UK are among the most well-known and paradigmatic examples of this ethos, although, it should be noted, the international

DIY community was, and is, composed of literally countless numbers of practitioners. These bands helped create an international community with its own record labels, distribution companies, venues, touring circuits, and fanzines. An entire self-sustaining network of DIY punk sprang up without the knowledge or the blessing of the mainstream culture industry. DIY punk created its own alternative arena in which, perhaps by necessity, values like mutual aid and cooperation became the norm.

In *We Jam Econo*, a documentary about the American punk rock band the Minutemen,[70] their singer and guitarist D. Boon states that "One of our philosophies in the Minutemen also has to do with that [...] there should be more interaction with music and everyday people, because that's what we are. [...] There should be a band on every block, there should be a nightclub on every other block, and a record label on every other block after that."[71] As their bass player Mike Watt elaborates in the next scene, "This idea that D. Boon had that working people should be able to go to gigs, so hey, 'Let's start the gig at 7:30, let's put it where you don't have to drive 30 miles each way.' This was intense. This wasn't like 'Let's do a showcase so we can get signed and be a rock band.' This wasn't in his sensibility at all."[72] D. Boon died tragically in a van accident in 1985, but Mike Watt has continued to write and perform music. He ends each performance by telling the audience, "Start your own band, paint your own picture, write your own book."

This idea—that the arts should be a radically decentralized, integral part of a community, and in the hands of anyone who wants to get involved—is a central notion in the ecological version of progress. Rather than being tied to show business and the capitalist marketplace, art should be focused on becoming a part of its community, working towards strengthening and improving that community. Rather than trying to "make it" in the mainstream culture industry, or the world of high art, an artist's goal should be to forge a better, stronger social order by bringing people together to collaborate and cooperate in the creation and production of their own culture.

THE LIMITS OF DIY

D. Boon's dreams for the decentralization of art seem somewhat different from the much more limited views endemic to the DIY punk community in which he operated. He seems to be aiming for much more direct community outreach and involvement than the often intentional marginalization prevalent in that scene. Boon's above remarks were made near the end of his 27 years, and he did not live to pursue them, so there is no way of knowing the exact details of what he had in mind. However, in these brief remarks, he seems to be expressing a desire to push out of the boundaries of the often hermetic world of underground punk.

The DIY values of the 80s hardcore punk scene in which the Minutemen operated offers an only limited form of cultural and political rebellion. As Stephen Duncombe writes, "Playing out a tradition of bohemian elitism, [...] the underground has learned to worship purity and obscurity. This is part of its romance, but also its tragic flaw."[73] By remaining small and managing its own affairs, DIY punk does not threaten or challenge the mainstream of the capitalist culture industry, rather, it simply avoids it. By embracing an obscurity-is-next-to-godliness ideal exemplified in the Germ's song "What We Do Is Secret," DIY punk merely succeeds at creating a small, tolerated fringe that can do its own thing, under the radar, and on its own terms. Such a movement, while valuable for its members, has relinquished the chance for any real socio-political impact by design. By remaining willfully marginalized, rather than creating larger, more permanent cultural institutions that might challenge and supplant corporate hegemony, the world of DIY punk has all-too-often been rendered nothing more than the research and development wing of the culture industry.

Of course, it would be grossly unfair to simply declare the DIY community the mainstream in microcosm. A different set of values tends to permeate the production and consumption of art and music throughout this underground. But these differing values can only accomplish so much. Unless stronger countercultural institutions can be created, the mainstream, endlessly trafficking in hype and hollowness, and peddling its perverted version of culture to every corner of the globe, will carry on, uninterrupted. Institutions that make truly powerful and transformative art available to everyone must be created, so that hopefully someday soon, we can all look back and wonder how anyone ever bought what the culture industry had to sell.

The deliberate hermeticism of DIY punk is reminiscent of Hakim Bey's TAZ (Temporary Autonomous Zone). Bey, an anarchist author with pronounced propensities toward both mysticism and impenetrable prose, posits his autonomous zones as temporary oases of freedom where a few people can briefly experience utopia and then merge back into society before they "get caught" being free. However ridiculous this may sound, especially when put forth as a politically significant idea, such an interpretation is not unfounded. As Bey himself writes, "The TAZ is like an uprising that does not engage directly with the state, a guerrilla operation which liberates an area (of land, of time, of imagination), and then dissolves itself elsewhere/elsewhen, *before* the state can crush it."[74] This willfully eccentric attempt to briefly escape repression, which neither challenges the sources of that repression, nor even *intends* to challenge them, can only achieve a very limited victory. It will do very few people very little good if there is periodically a short-lived oasis of freedom. Similarly, DIY punk's acceptance of its role as an accepted fringe that fails to confront the existing system simply allows for the existence of a subcultural oasis with inherently limited membership and inherently limited impact.

Stronger, more lasting, and far more inclusive alternative cultural institutions need to exist. These should, most importantly, be willing to directly challenge and confront existing institutions. Subcultures and temporary autonomous zones may be thrilling places to hide and play, but if we wish to challenge the irrational systems surrounding us, it will be necessary to come out of hiding. This call for larger, more powerful alternative cultural institutions is not a demand for more of what has happened with a number of DIY labels, such as Merge Records from Chapel Hill, North Carolina. Merge began in the late 1980s, releasing 7" singles whose covers were hand-folded at the owners' homes, but now releases albums that have topped the Billboard charts. While Merge's undiminished punk rock ethos in the face of this success and continued dedication to releasing interesting music is admirable, this sort of growth is not the ideal. The goal should not be to compete with the culture industry at its own game, but to create an entirely different game with a different set of rules. The culture industry will not be destroyed by participating in it. A true alternative must exist. In order to succeed, these new cultural institutions will need to be formed in parallel with more conventionally political institutions that can similarly challenge the hegemony of our existing irrational power structures with a socially rational system.

Although art can, in may ways, work in advance of politics, probing the limits of the possible and transforming minds to create a new citizenry that can wisely wield the powers of these new systems, it is crucial that the parallel political projects do not lag far behind, lest these new cultural institutions are simply relegated to the dustbin of subculture-hood, while the same old systems grind destructively along. This very unfortunate possibility would be rendered inevitable without the at least somewhat simultaneous reconstruction of art and society. As was mentioned earlier, art *can* work in advance of politics, but it ought not be left alone on the frontier for long, forced into eventual irrelevance by its solitude.

SOCIAL SCULPTURE AND SOCIAL ECOLOGY

We need new institutions, both cultural and political. But how would these new institutions function? How would they be structured? Part of the answer to these questions was addressed with both Joseph Beuys' social sculpture, and the previously mentioned work of Murray Bookchin, who similarly sought to create fully democratic structures that function on a face-to-face basis. Both men had a great deal more in mind concerning democracy than the common notion that we need an active electorate that turns out at the polls and performs its civic duties with pride. Bookchin harkened back to the model of active citizenship exemplified by the Athenian polis. It should be noted that Bookchin refused to lose sight of the fact that Athens was a slave-owning society, and those slaves, along with women and resident aliens, were not allowed to participate in the public realm. Athens is thus not an ideal to recreate, but simply proof that the nation-state is not our only option in governance. It is not only *theoretically possible* for community members to meet in a face-to-face forum to set policies and make political decisions, but *it has been done*. Even more importantly, *it worked*.

Politics derives etymologically from the Greek *polis*, meaning "city." *Polis* is often translated as "city-state," but the conflation of Athens' municipal democracy with the centralized, hierarchical structure of a nation-state is a piece of ideological baggage foisted onto an institution where it does not belong. With an eye toward its etymology, Bookchin writes, "Politics, almost by definition, *is* the active engagement of citizens in the handling of their municipal affairs and in their defense of its freedom."[75] Bookchin made the essential distinction between politics and statecraft. Statecraft emerged from the impulse to dominate and exploit the citizenry through a hierarchical, centralized apparatus in an ultimately successful drive to supplant the political power of that citizenry. Politics ought to be what happens on the local level between citizens who seek to manage and control their own affairs.

Bookchin referred to his body of ideas as "social ecology." He persuasively posited the notion that our ecological problems are, at root, social ones. As was discussed above, the same domination and hierarchy driving our social world fuels the destruction of the natural world. Nature is not valued as an end in itself—to be respected, preserved and utilized wisely—but is a means to another end, namely, profit. Just as all human relationships have been reduced to market-based, mutually antagonistic exchanges, so too is nature subsumed under the demands of the market. Forests are bulldozed if it is good for business. The natural world becomes simply another rung on a ladder of hierarchical relationships where servility and obedience, rather than equality and cooperation, are expected all the way down. So not only does our current social situation fuel an *understanding* of nature that reflects the dominant ideology, but our social situation also forces the natural world to *join in* the machinations of that ideology. As Bookchin states, "The imbalances man has produced in the natural world are caused by the imbalances he has produced in the social world."[76] Joseph Beuys similarly felt that our ecological problems have social causes and social solutions. After discussing the illness of our social organism, he stated, "It is also difficult for people to grasp the criteria for the need for institutions, for measures that must be taken. This [the creation of new social institutions] would be ecology if we could grasp this ecological question at its root."[77]

The natural world's only hope is also humanity's. Centralization, hierarchy, and market-based relationships need to be rendered a relic of the past. Face-to-face, democratic structures operating on a community level need to be created. This possibility still remains open. As Bookchin states, "Impure as they may be, there are still areas of life—notably, the municipalities—that can be reclaimed by an active citizenry in popular assemblies, confederated, and ultimately developed into a counterpower with counterinstitutions that stand opposed to the nation-state."[78]

Furthermore, the root causes of our artistic problems, our ecological problems, and our social problems are basically identical. In each case, the antagonism, competition, and desire to dominate that permeates our market-based world creates an unhealthy and untenable state of affairs. In each case, non-hierarchical, decentralized systems that operate on a sensible human scale, and treat *everything*—from humans, to art, to nature—as an end in itself, rather than a means to a profit, are our only hope.

ART, ENLIGHTENMENT, AND CITIZENSHIP

The reconstruction of the arts plays a central role in this overall project, as there exists a perplexing conundrum that faces anyone who seeks to create a more just and rational world. The conundrum is this: We need an enlightened and reformed citizenry to create and maintain just and rational social institutions, yet it is difficult to have an enlightened and reformed citizenry without just and rational social institutions. So how can the process of recreating humanity and society begin? Art, by becoming a true avant-garde, can provide new ways of seeing, being, and understanding. It can point the way out of the limitations of the present, and help create an enlightened citizenry capable of creating and maintaining a just and rational social structure.

New cultural institutions need to be formed. Rather than accepting market-based approaches that see art and artists as the means to a profitable end, we need institutions that value art as art, as a valuable addition to our shared cultural life that can create new modes of seeing and understanding. Rather than seeking to climb the ladders of the culture industry or high art, artists need to focus on providing meaningful works for the collective life of a functioning community. High art must be democratized. Creativity must be spread. The culture industry must be destroyed.

BEGINNING AGAIN

Our current situation—in the arts, in politics, and in our treatment of the natural world—has reached a crisis of magnificent proportions. We ought to create new cultural and political institutions based on new fundamental concepts and new modes of being. As Murray Bookchin writes in his essay "Listen, Marxist!": "Either we will shed the past—in ourselves and in our groups—or there will be no future to win."[79] In short, we need to develop a new citizenry that can tackle our countless crises creatively and cooperatively.

But where will this new citizenry come from? How can we create new institutions in a world filled with minds molded by the old institutions? If we are to finally break free from the strictures of the present, there must be some understanding of what could be, of what a human life could entail, and of how a society could function. In John Dewey's conception, art is the creative reordering of the materials of the world into a meaningful, satisfactory form. By creating new forms and new ideas, art plays a potentially powerful role in awakening humanity to as-yet unexplored possibilities. Many of the new ideas we need can be developed and disseminated through the arts.

Yet postmodernists would have us believe that it is impossible to escape the confines of the present. We have reached the end of art, nay, the end of history. The market has won, and all anyone can do is rehash the past, running forever in place in a wonderland of consumption. But is this really the case? Thankfully, no. When Arthur Danto declares that art history has reached its end, and further decrees that only genre exercises from bygone eras are possible from now until forever, he fails to take into account, unlike Joseph Beuys, the incredible potential held by humanity's creative drive. All Danto *really* manages to do is place the final period on the modernists' reductive and unrealistic version of art history. Warhol's *Brillo Boxes* do not actually mark the end of art, but rather, the end of the intricately woven historical fiction spun by the modernists.

The ideal definition of artistic progress is quite unlike the version created by the modernists and deemed complete by the postmodernists. Rather than a single arc that follows specific formal developments, a more useful understanding of artistic progress consists in the creation of a tangled web of interlocking and unique stories. Our understanding of artistic progress ought to mirror progress as it exists in the natural world. In both an advanced art world and a thriving ecosystem, there exists a wealth of diversity, in which unique elements contribute to a thriving, complex whole. Both Joseph Beuys and John Cage are notable not only for their unique, idiosyncratic, and highly individual works, but for the egalitarian social elements present in these works. Both men were able to construct a unique artistic vocabulary without retreating into disengaged hermeticism. Both sought to turn their personal artistic discoveries into political propositions available to everyone. Their work is a potent example of how the arts could function. The individual is free to develop in unique ways while simultaneously engaging with, and contributing to, the greater social organism.

ART AND POLITICS

The arts are currently presented as commodities that allow for a disengagement from reality, rather than a meaningful engagement with the world, or a worthwhile attempt to capture what it means to be a human being. Art is offered as a means for unwinding and taking it easy, not a source for changing one's understanding. As the novelist David Foster Wallace said of television, in a statement that could easily be applied to the vast majority of the art and culture that currently surrounds us:

> I think one of the insidious lessons about TV is the meta-lesson that you're dumb. This is all you can do. This is easy, and you're

> the sort of person who really just wants to sit in a chair and have it easy. When in fact, there are parts of us, in a way, that are a lot more ambitious than that. And what we need [...] is seriously engaged art that can teach again that we're smart.[80]

We are too smart to live in a world structured like our current one. Just as everyone is, at least potentially, an artist, everyone is also potentially smart enough to not only *imagine* a better world, but to collectively bring it into being. Seriously engaged art can play an incredible role in alerting us to our latent intelligence and creativity, which is our true capital, and our most valuable resource. We need art that can affirm this, art made for the purpose of creating, sustaining, and refining a better social order.

If we are to create such art, the manner in which we create and distribute culture must change. Art must not be an escape or diversion from life, but an encounter with it. This will only be possible if both the capitalist culture industry and the museumified world of high art are replaced as the main sources of our shared cultural experiences. Both high art and the culture industry place art *into* communities from the outside. But art ought to be created from *within* the context of the day-to-day life of increasingly decentralized communities. Only then could art truly contribute to the shared cultural life of those communities, acting as a source of new ideas and new modes of understanding.

This reclamation and reconstruction of the arts plays a key role in a larger political and ecological project that aims at the eventual dissolution of the nation-state in favor of decentralized, directly democratic institutions.

How can the arts contribute to this process? First, and perhaps most obviously, our cultural institutions can be one among many institutions seized and controlled by local communities, thus ignoring and hopefully crippling the centralized cultural apparatuses that currently fill our world with almost invariably over-hyped and unfulfilling artworks. Second, the arts can change minds and impact lives in truly profound ways, thus laying the groundwork for future political progress by creating new notions of what is possible. This is a vision of art as a true avant-garde, scouting the perimeter for new ideas and new directions. Third, by making creativity part of the shared experience of a community, rather than some mysterious act that happens elsewhere and is packaged, shipped, and sold, the act of creation becomes a process that can be engaged in by anyone and everyone. Joseph Beuys' notion that everyone is an artist could become common sense. Any act worth doing can be executed creatively, artistically, and in a way that creates something new, meaningful, and perhaps, socially useful. The potential impact of such a transformation in our understanding of creativity should not be underestimated.

The rejection of art's present state is not simply a rejection, but an *affirmation* of its possible future, and by extension, humanity's future. An overhaul of the arts ought to be but one portion of a larger political and ecological project that aims toward the total decentralization and democratization of every institution. This overall project is humanity's only real hope to end domination against one another and the natural world. The role of the arts in this project is vital. The arts can create and disseminate new fundamental concepts, and can provide an experiential taste of other modes of being, thus allowing people to understand what could be if we could only get to work making it exist. Most importantly, now is the time to begin. If we do not begin this project, and begin it immediately, there may soon be nothing left to save.

Q.E.D.

NOTES

1 Leo Tolstoy, *The Kingdom of God Is Within You and What Is Art?* (New York: Charles Scribner's Sons, 1900), p. 517.
2 Paul Morley, "On gospel, Abba and the death of the record: an audience with Brian Eno," *The Observer*, January 17, 2010.
3 Ben Sisario, "Looking to a Sneaker For a Band's Big Break," *The New York Times*, October 10, 2010, *Arts & Leisure*, p. 1.
4 Yes, *that* Nike.
5 After first writing about this new corporate involvement in music, it has become nearly impossible for me to read about "independent" music without encountering mention of this phenomenon. This either signifies that my corporate-sponsored-music radar has been activated

or that this trend is becoming more prevalent. In a single session on the internet, I first followed a link to an intriguing band's website, only to find that their most recent piece of news was a photo shoot they had done for the clothing company J Crew, complete with links to the company's website. Troubled, and no longer intrigued, I navigated away to another music site, only to see that the top story of the day involved two of the most lauded bands of the moment collaborating on a Christmas song for the department store Target. The story was simply one of reportage. No qualms were registered. Instead there were links for downloading the song from Target's website.

6 My paraphrase of Wittgenstein here is intentional. There is a great similarity between Cage's use of form and the later work of Wittgenstein, in particular, with the shared notion that meaning is determined by use.

7 John Dewey, *Art As Experience* (New York: Perigee Books, 1980), p. 7.

8 Ibid, p. 14.

9 Ibid, p. 35.

10 Ibid, p. 65. Emphasis in original.

11 Ibid, p. 68.

12 Ibid.

13 Ibid., p. 39.

14 Phil Mariana, ed., *Joseph Beuys* (New York: Dia Art Foundation, 1987), pp. 24-5.

15 Many of Beuys' interpreters treat him as a mostly humorless figure with a drive toward quasi-mystical shamanism, but this work, like many of his others is really quite humorous and playful. Which is also of

course not to say that Beuys was a joke or a sham artist, pulling one over on the art world. Many humorous works are dead serious, a great example being the film *Dr Strangelove or: How I learned to Stop Worrying and Love the Bomb*, one of the greatest anti-war films ever made, as well as an absolute riot.

16 This notion of the head as the locus of new ideas is something of an oversimplification of the actual nature of human thought. Following someone like Daniel Dennett and the notion of "embodied cognition," it seems safe to assert that thoughts are generated from much more than just the head, but rather, from the entire organism's interaction with the world. The point here is not the scientific accuracy of Beuys' analogy, but the message behind it.

17 Though a central aspect of Beuys' self-mythologizing, there is some debate as to whether or not this story is true. I have not personally looked at the details of the debate enough to have a firm opinion one way or the other, and will simply accept Beuys' account as true.

18 Beyond their roots in his biography, fat and felt are also key elements, on a purely formal level, in his sculptures. Rather than fixed, solid objects, sculptures composed of fat and felt are soft and malleable. Fat in particular is prone to change over time in relation to fluctuations in temperature.

19 Volker Harlan, ed., *What Is Art? Conversations With Joseph Beuys*, (Forest Row, UK: Clairview, 2007), pp. 21-2.

20 Ibid., p. 27.

21 Dewey, *Art As Experience*, p. 81.

22 Richard Kostelanetz, ed., *Conversing With Cage* (New York: Routeledge, 2003, 2nd ed.), p. 241.
23 The questions are italicized. Cage's answers are in roman. No capital letters or punctuation are used, although I have added capitalization and punctuation to the following passage to facilitate easier reading.
24 John Cage, *I-VI* (Cambridge, Massachusetts: Harvard University Press, 1990), pp. 176-8.
25 John Cage, *Silence* (Hanover, New Hampshire: Wesleyan University Press, 1961), p. 10.
26 Glenn Branca, *Indeterminate Activity of Resultant Masses* (Atavistic Records, Compact Disc, 2007).
27 Cage, *Silence*, p. 64.
28 Ibid, p. 65.
29 James Pritchett, *The Music of John Cage* (Cambridge, Massachusetts: Cambridge University Press, 1993), p. 160.
30 Ibid, p. 108.
31 Ibid, p. 137.
32 Kostelanetz, *Conversing With Cage*, p. 273.
33 Richard Kostelanetz, *On Innovative Art(ist)s: Recollections of an Expanding Field* (Jefferson, North Carolina: McFarland & Company, 1992), p. 232.
34 Ibid, p. 231.
35 Harlan, *What Is Art?*, p. 14.
36 Andreas Huyssen, *After the Great Divide: Modernism, Mass Culture, Postmodernism* (Bloomington, Indiana: Indiana University Press, 1986), p. 56.
37 Frederic Jameson, *Postmodernism, or, The Cultural Logic of Late Capitalism* (Durham, North Carolina: Duke University Press, 1991), p. 2.

38 Clement Greenberg, *The Collected Essays and Criticism: Volume 1* (Chicago: University of Chicago Press, 1986), p. 11.
39 Ibid, p. 12.
40 For Greenberg. Someone like Andreas Huyssen makes a distinction between the two. I would tend to side with Huyssen on this one.
41 Clement Greenberg, *Late Writings* (Minneapolis: University of Minnesota Press, 2003), p. 30-31.
42 Ibid, pp. 32-33.
43 Ibid, p. 30.
44 Arthur Danto, *Beyond the Brillo Box* (Berkeley: University of California Press, 1992) p. 10.
45 Ibid.
46 Greenberg, *Late Writings* p. 61.
47 Danto, *Beyond the Brillo Box* p. 10.
48 Ibid, p. 42.
49 Ibid p. 41.
50 For him, it is the art object's ability to embody and signify meaning. For Dewey, it is the art object's ability to create *an* experience. For our purposes here, we'll just assume that this amounts to pretty much the same thing. It is, at the very least, safe to say that both men would agree that an artwork's meaning is historically contingent.
51 Theodor Adorno, *Prisms* (Cambridge, Massachusetts: MIT Press, 1983) p. 123.
52 Ibid, pp. 124-125.
53 Jameson, *Postmodernism*, p. 48.
54 Ibid, p. 305.
55 Ibid, p. 63.

56 Ibid, p. 64.
57 Greenberg, *Collected Essays and Criticism*, p. 13.
58 Ibid.
59 William Rubin, ed., "*Primitivism in 20th Century Art: Affinity of the Tribal and the Modern* (New York: Museum of Modern Art, 1984), p. 242.
60 Ibid.
61 Bernard Gendron, *Popular Music and the Avant-Garde: Between Montmartre and the Mudd Club* (Chicago: University of Chicago Press, 2002), p. 2.
62 Ibid, p. 29.
63 Ibid, p. 3.
64 Murray Bookchin, *The Ecology of Freedom, The Emergence and Dissolution of Hierarchy* (Palo Alto, California: Cheshire Books, 1982), p. 24. Emphasis in original.
65 Although, with the recent rise of the chef-as-rock-star-phenomenon, this may soon become a reality.
66 Bookchin, *The Ecology of Freedom*, p. 24. Emphasis in original.
67 In what follows, I am indebted to the work of Murray Bookchin.
68 Penny Rimbaud, *Shibboleth: My Revolting Life* (Oakland, CA: AK Press, 1998), p. 74.
69 Ibid.
70 It is interesting to note a way in which the Minutemen utilized a technique that echoes the Cagean use of formal elements to make political points. D. Boon intentionally kept his guitar amp set to play almost solely treble, with the mid ranges and low end filtered out. His goal was to

have the bass, drums, and guitars inhabit separate realms, as sovereign kingdoms of sound that would not interfere with one another. So what the listener hears are three very distinct instruments playing sonically separated parts that all contribute to a single song.

71 Tim Irwin, dir., *We Jam Econo: The Story of the Minutemen* (Plexifilm, DVD, 2006).

72 Ibid.

73 Stephen Duncombe, *Notes From Underground: Zines and the Politics of Alternative Culture* (New York: Verso, 1997), p. 168.

74 Hakim Bey, *T.A.Z. The Temporary Autonomous Zone* (New York: Autonomedia, 1991), p.99.

75 Murray Bookchin, *Social Ecology and Communalism* (Oakland, CA: AK Press, 2007), p. 94. Emphasis in original.

76 Murray Bookchin, *Post-Scarcity Anarchism* (Oakland, CA: AK Press, 2004), p. 33.

77 Harlan, *What Is Art?*, p. 22.

78 Bookchin, *Post-Scarcity Anarchism*, p. xxxiv.

79 Ibid., p. 143.

80 David Lipsky, *Although of course you end up becoming yourself: a road trip with David Foster Wallace* (New York: Broadway Books, 2010), p. 71.

Printed in Great Britain
by Amazon